COLOR OF THE CROSS

Based on the screenplay
COLOR OF THE CROSS

Written by
AYVEE VERZONILLA

Story by
JEAN CLAUDE LAMARRE

This book is dedicated to the most creative woman I hardly knew, my mother- rest in peace.

ACKNOWLEDGEMENTS

First and foremost, I would like to thank the Higher Power for guiding and protecting me in all ways. I am so very grateful for my wonderful siblings and cousins who have been here for me throughout my creative journey: Christopher, Josie, Jeremy, Zen, Orvin, Jeffrey and future superstar Miss Sencere, my favorite niece. Radha Nilia, you are a visionary and filmmaker of this generation. Without you I am lost and I mean it!

I would also like to thank Maya Verzonilla for opening up my world and heart to all things that were once in darkness. Your words and advice have never gone in one ear and out of the other!

To my friend, amateur editor and close confidante Erica, whose late night conversations and "real talk" have kept me going when times were less than perfect, you are my heart. Karin, it's always been you and I poolside, and don't you forget it. Marvin, you are a life -saver!

To my best friend and love of my life, Talon Miles, whose belief in my potential is unfaltering: I simply could not have done this without your support.

Lastly, I would like to thank my mentor, Jean Claude Lamarre, for taking a chance on a young girl and allowing me to expand and flourish. Given this opportunity, I've been able to accomplish a feat greater than I had dared to even imagine. You have been a blessing in my life.

COLOR OF THE CROSS

TABLE OF CONTENTS

*	PROLOGUE
1	HUNTED
2	THE OPEN ROAD
3	A VERY CLOSE CALL
4	THE FATHER HAS SPOKEN
5	TWO MESSENGERS
6	PASSOVER
7	A TRAITOR IS REVEALED
8	DANGER
9	AN UNLIKELY FRIENDSHIP
10	SATAN BEGONE
11	THE START OF TEMPTATION
12	DELIRIUM
13	IT HAS BEGUN
14	THE DREAM
15	WHAT LIES AHEAD?
16	BEFORE I COULD SEE
17	SPREAD THE WORD
18	JOURNEYING ON
19	THE TWO HOUSES
20	CORNERED
21	ALL HAIL CAESAR
22	THE AGONY OF JOSHUA
23	THE CRUCIFIXION OF A KING
24	THE MESSIAH LIVES

We should all know diversity makes for a rich tapestry, and we must understand that all the threads of the tapestry are equal in value no matter what their color.

Maya Angelou

FOREWORD by Jean Claude LaMarre

A black Jesus? What is the social relevance of this issue? Does it really matter what color his skin was? Won't it serve to polarize Christians? Is this a racist view? These are all questions that I have encountered along my journey toward making this important film. And like Magneto, the superhero, who only gains more strength in equal proportion to the resistance he encounters, these questions have only served to help strengthen my understanding of just how important putting another face on the religious figure we all have come to know as Jesus Christ is.

Much of the resistance I've encountered, and sometimes anger, have come from Christians themselves, who in their minds are only protecting a symbol very near and sacred to their hearts. But like the pro-lifer, who bombs the abortion clinic because he believes that's how he can best save lives, it goes against the very thing they are fighting to protect. In fact, because we're Christians, it shouldn't matter that Jesus is portrayed as black, *which is the very reason he should be portrayed as black*. How can we claim to believe and accept his message of love - a message that was all inclusive and universal, yet reserve his image to just one race. Christians exist on every continent from Africa to Europe. We cannot be selective Christians in our portrayal of Jesus, as we look to broaden his appeal, while spreading his message.

Leonardo Davinci committed no great crime in portraying Jesus as a blonde hair, blue eyed man. He merely took a revered figure, one that most likely didn't look like him, and painted him in a manner that made the figure more accessible to his fellow Italian countrymen. In other words, he Europeanized Jesus for those Europeans who loved Jesus. For this Davinci should be applauded. He understood that worship and Faith can be best achieved, with any religion, not through foreign symbols or images, but through ideas and images that stem from and look like us.

PROLOGUE

Joshua, a young boy of about age ten, stands staring blankly at the retreating figures of two light-skinned Jewish boys, running at break neck speed. His hair and clothes are disheveled and an ugly, raised bruise has begun to form underneath his left eye. He turns to gaze at a man in the background who holds a pouch of newly purchased carpentry tools in his arms. The man quickly approaches Joshua.

"Are those boys bullying you again?" he asks in a low, hushed tone.

Joshua looks down, his eyes a whirl of mist and confusion. He fights the burning sting of tears with a noncommittal shrug of his shoulders. The man places one hand on Joshua's arm comfortingly and sighs, frustrated.

"Why must I be so different from the others, and why do they hate me so?" the boy asks innocently.

The man kneels down, fixing his gaze solemnly on the boy.

"Joshua, I know being the Son of God is not easy. This will not be the last time people will envy your talents or persecute you for being a Black Jew. You must always remember that your gift is a blessing and one day, you will grow to save the nations.

Joshua smiles, heartened by these words… He looks up at the sky and speaks to the heavens.

"I will always remember to speak your words Father, and I will never be ashamed of the color of my skin."

HUNTED Chapter 1

It is evening. I am cold, tired and frightened. I have not slept in two days. We have been traveling across the mountainside for many hours, with very little time for rest. Finally, we have reached a clearing, and set up camp. I have journeyed long and hard and seen much more than a man should see on this day.

Yet, I cannot sleep.

And as the fateful hour that my Master speaks so frequently of nears, I wonder if I will ever sleep again. I look around the campfire to see Peter, Matthew, Simon and John all wide awake; their eyes hollow, wandering aimlessly, lit only by the full moon. The quiet night is deceptive in its peacefulness.

We all know this.

My Master, the dark-skinned Nazareen known as Joshua, has drifted off into the night. To insure that he is safe, James has followed him several yards from where we have set up camp, beyond a rocky bend. In this clearing, my Master will spend hours, as he does so frequently, in prayer and meditation, alone.

He refers to these moments as "conversations" with his father. During these exchanges, we must never disturb him. Not that he has ever told us this directly, but you would understand if you spent even a moment in his presence why he must be left alone. The joy he experiences after these conversations radiates something so powerful, that we dare not interrupt this divine interplay between Father and Son. Their communication can sometimes last for hours at a time while we wait.

One evening, it was my turn to stand and watch over him while he prayed. I observed in silence while the moonlit sky shone down on him, and he uttered words in a language that my ears could not understand. After these utterances, he waited respectfully for what I gathered was a response from his Father above.

Suddenly, a burst of radiant moonlight beamed down upon my Master, and a smile formed on his face. His Father was responding. They continued this exchange for hours while I watched, transfixed.

Tonight, somehow is different.

But to better understand what has brought us here, and why our lives are in danger, you have to understand who we are.

I am one of twelve of his close followers. We are called Disciples. We are the trusted followers of Joshua of Nazareth, the Son of God, the Messiah foretold in the scriptures. We are diverse men, both in background and skin tone, connected to a common cause: telling everyone we encounter about the glory of the kingdom of heaven!

My Master's beliefs directly challenge the creed of the Torah. Professing his teachings make us blasphemers in the eyes of the Sanhedrin. We are marked men who are thought to be evil and by law must be imprisoned. Many declare we must be put to death. As we go about spreading the words of my Master, we are hunted night and day by rabbis, Roman guards, and anyone else who is afraid of hearing the truth and its power.

There is only one true path to everlasting life and that is through Him.

THE OPEN ROADS Chapter 2

When I first set eyes upon my Master, I was fascinated with this man. His integrity drew me in, made me yearn for understanding and enlightenment, and his words brought wisdom and excitement to my unchallenged mind. Once I accepted him, it was if I was born again.

As soon as his kind voice summoned me, I immediately left my humble duties as a fisherman to support a higher cause. Instinct told me that my life would never be the same again.

I was right....

Among a multitude of other gifts, he granted His Disciples the ability to perform certain miracles. In the short years that I traveled with my Master, I brought sight to a woman who had been robbed of vision since birth; I straightened the legs of a lame man, and brought a young child back from beyond death. To perform these healings took a great deal of time, energy, and faith in my Master and the Father.

At times, my faith wavered but, it was miraculous to both see and bestow these blessings.

I speak of this not to brag or boast about myself, but only to proclaim the glory of the Messiah who worked through me. My Master taught his Disciples never to seek acceptance or glory from the eyes of men, but to do good deeds in silence and receive our reward in heaven. To my Master, the humblest of men was greater than the richest and most awarded.

But there were many men I saw along our journey who would seek glory and acceptance from the people around them. They would pray in open view of a large crowd, proclaim their undying devotion for the Torah and the Father, or show generosity just to look honorable in front of their peers.

There was one teacher we met along our travels who deeply desired to be a Disciple. He pulled my Master aside and proclaimed his undying love for the Messiah. He told my Master that he was willing to follow him wherever he would lead, from that moment on. My Master declined the scholar's offer because he believed the man sought fame and exaltation from his students and neighbors.

Before being led here, Joshua of Nazareth was a carpenter, and had chosen men from all walks of life to be his Disciples. Matthew was a tax collector. Peter, a huge bear of a man, was a fisherman like James and John, while Matthew was the eldest. Others of us were farmers and shepherds. A fair amount of us are well educated, while others work best with their hands.

We are as all men and women in Judea: very mixed. The intermingling of cultures has caused us to be made up of all colors and all levels of success. As for me, Thomas, I had been a prosperous fisherman in my life before meeting my Master. It was a life that seems now as distant to me as the mountains of Asia, or the great Caspian Sea. The thought of how far we have come, runs through my mind, as we make our way along the open roads.

Whenever we travel, I always make sure to walk near the back of the group. I feel protected back there, where I can watch the other men. I wonder how my their faith can be so strong when I question mine moment by moment. As we walk, I strive to douse the uncertainty that wears on my soul.

Joshua is always out in front, leading us, always laughing and talking with his best friend, Peter. There is a calmness and peacefulness about him that infects us all. Bartholomew, Thaddeus, Andrew, Matthew, and Simon usually walk in a group together, offering up prayers or melodic passages. Timothy almost always walks by himself. Others move from group to group. All look as if they carry more of a sense of purpose than I. Of all the Disciples, I am probably closest to the youngest of us, John. When we camp, he and I share a tent, and have found comfort and joy in one another's company.

A VERY CLOSE CALL Chapter 3

We continue to walk at a slow pace, beaten down by the torturous heat. My robes are tattered and dusty. My skin itches from dust mites and countless insects. My throat cries out for water. I must admit that I am near spent, and after assessing the others, they do not seem too far behind me.

I look down at my feet: swollen, blistered and sore. I am amazed that despite this abuse, my body never ceases to be inspired by my Master's words and keeps moving. I only hope my spirit is as certain about Joshua's message. Why do I sometimes doubt my Master, after all that I had been taught and seen? I longed to have the unwavering faith that some of my brothers, like Peter, displayed.

I always look out for John during our travels because he is of a slight, almost female build. He and I are trailing behind the others, deep in thought, when we are suddenly startled by the unmistakable hoof beats and jangling chains of Roman chariots. Danger approaches.

My heart starts to race as we hear the scraping and bumping sound of heavy wooden wheels against the dirt and stones in the road. We glance fearfully at one another and then, look immediately to Joshua for his orders.

Romans! Many of them! Driving chariots! My heart continues to race. Joshua motions and waves us toward the thick brush only a short distance from the road where we can hide. We start running for cover, but are stopped by a shout from the betrayer, Judas, who draws his sword and calls on us all to battle the oncoming Romans.

"We cannot let the Romans come into our land and treat us Jews like dogs," shouts Judas.

The Messiah asks Judas if, after he has defeated the approaching Romans, does he plan on taking up arms against the entire Roman army, because surely that is what an enemy of Rome would have to do.

We all knew the Roman army would not stand by and let eight of its men be ambushed without seeking vengeance in return. John and I watch quietly while Joshua and Judas engage one another. Only Peter, who had sworn to defend Joshua at all costs, stays in the open with the two men.

Much of Judea was over run by Romans who, in their murderous siege of land worldwide, took over nearby Syria nearly sixty years ago. Soon after, since we could do little to stop them, they seized Judea as well. Most of us lived under their occupation our entire lives.

We abhorred having our country occupied by these animals and would do almost anything to hasten their retreat. Judas was among a large number who felt the only way to end the Roman occupation was to drive them out by taking up arms against them. They were tired of waiting for someone else to come and rescue us, and sought freedom by force if necessary. Judas and other Jews who supported this opinion were part of a group called the Zealots.

Joshua's solution could not have been more different. It was a motion of faith, prayer, and surrender to a higher power. He let all of his troubles be taken care of by the Father, willingly. Joshua reminded Judas of this, that violence was not the way.

The Zealots are fueled by their passion for vengeance. I have two close friends who are Zealots, Avraham and Yona, two elderly Jews. Beyond friendship, I think of them as a mother and father. They are an honest and humble couple, wanting no more than to live and die peacefully of old age.

The vile Roman soldiers decided to harass them as they were walking home from the market carrying some food for the Seder Feast of the Passover holiday. It sickens me to say that Horatius, the largest and (reputedly the cruelest) of the Roman centurions, happened upon them.

Without cause, he grabbed Avraham by the neck and flung him face first into the dirt, spilling his food and humiliating him in front of his wife. This was the straw that broke the camels back for him, and it was so close to the sacred Passover!

A proud man, Avraham muttered under his breath as Yona helped him up from the ground, "A dog with a sword is still a dog."

Horatius drew his sword and put it to Avraham's skinny, frail throat so tightly that Yona later showed me a cloth soaked in blood she had held against his throat to save his life.

Such confrontations occur night and day throughout Judea. Jews young and old face death if they dare to speak up against the Romans or their occupation of our land. It is no wonder that a large number of them side with Judas and would gladly take up the sword against them.

There were days when I was among that number.

Today was such a day that I would have taken up arms alongside Judas, the Zealot, but I was afraid to come out from my hiding place behind the bushes and stand with him. I cannot say if I was more afraid of the Roman soldiers or of the disappointment of my Master in watching me side with violence.

Finally, Joshua convinces Judas to lay down his arms. And for several moments, we watched the chariots and their cargo of Centurion guards ride past us. Four huge fighting machines were each carrying two Centurions, dressed in brightly polished battle armor!

On each chariot, one guard drives the two muscular, black horses by cracking a long, ornate whip above them, while the other brandishes his golden sword, held high in the air. I tremble uncontrollably, and I know my knees are rattling together so loudly that my brothers can hear them.

I am terror-stricken by the sight of so many guards!

I realize at that moment that Judas is a complete fool. The Romans had taken control of our country, most of Judea, heading all the way back to the Kidron Valley. They laid waste to dozens of armies without a second thought or semblance of remorse to the destruction they left behind. They were cold, effective and unstoppable. To attempt to defeat them in battle was to face certain death.

But as we watch the danger of the chariots disappear, as men are apt to do, I join with many of the Disciples in taunting the Roman soldiers.

Simon says, "If the Messiah hadn't made us hide in the bushes, we could have easily defeated those eight, puny soldiers; using only the three swords that were among us, the stones on the ground, and the element of surprise!"

We regale each other with stories of bravery, engaging in bloody battle, and achieving a wondrous victory for all of Judea! We boast of facing down all eight Centurions, but I doubt if I could have faced even one.

Today was truly a close call.

THE FATHER HAS SPOKEN Chapter 4

Our journey takes us along a seemingly endless road through countryside with few trees and almost no places to stop and rest. Finally, Joshua brings us all to a rise on the hillside above Arimathea, a small town we had all visited several times before. Many of us have friends in the area, and members of Joshua's family also live there. But this visit is different. When Joshua stops and we all gather to look down on Arimathea, my Master's face grows solemn. He looks more serious than I have ever seen him.

"Tomorrow," says Joshua. "I will be delivered here."

This causes an immediate uproar among us. None of us can believe that my Master would allow himself to be turned over to the rabbis. We argued with him, saying that surely we would not allow him to be delivered on any day, let alone the Passover. The feast is sacred and rabbis would never violate this High Holy Day. And if his detractors did try to seize him, we all vowed we would defend him to our deaths.

But, a part of me knew, as I stood watching him, that he was right. He is the Son of God, the Messiah. The Father had spoken his plans to Joshua in one of their conversations, and he knew what was going to happen.

It is a very dark moment for us and I search my memory for a motivational parable to reassure my Master. Unfortunately, very little comes to mind. Can you imagine the anguish of knowing that the Messiah will be put to death on the very next day? Some of us are hard pressed to continue. We want our time with our Master to last forever. But that, of course, cannot be.

John takes the news very badly. He collapses on the ground, telling our Master that he cannot bear to continue. Like a wife in mourning of her dead husband, he cries up to the heavens, convinced that his body is in too much pain and his heart is broken.

To have been blessed to be among our Master's Disciples was to be in a family. Joshua was our father, our leader, and our friend. The other

Disciples were truly brothers to me. Peter had a knack for making the best out of any situation. He is also a jokester and infamous prankster, as is our Master.

As disheartening as the confession was, Peter and the Messiah knew exactly how to bring us out of our premature bemoaning.

Peter, quick as can be, reaches down and snatches John up from the ground tossing him over his shoulder like a sack of milled flour! John is screaming and kicking his legs, pounding on Peter's back. Peter ignores him and catches our Master's eye with his. Joshua's expression is that of a mischievous grin, a face that he shares with few others than his Disciples. Peter knows, as we all do, that our Master has given him his blessing to continue with the journey.

"Perhaps I should carry this young woman down to Arimathea, for she is far too frail and weak to walk," he laughs.

"I think you're right! You have my blessing!"

Being mocked by our Master causes John's howls to increase. His voice reaches a high-pitched tone that is not unlike that of a little girl's outburst.

This is more than we can take!

As heartbroken as we are, we cannot hold back from uproarious laughter.

I begin laughing louder and harder at that moment than I have ever laughed in my life. It takes only a glance from my Master at John to make him chuckle as well.

We retell that moment to each other for several hours and prolong the laughter far longer than we would have under normal circumstances. It is exactly what we need at this time to inspire us to continue.

TWO MESSENGERS Chapter 5

The sun was setting and there was still a day's walk ahead of us, so my Master sent Paul to scout for a suitable place to make camp. All of us were concerned with whether we would safely passage into Arimathea the next day. With the Romans in power, and many of the rabbis considering us blasphemers, entering the city without warning could be very dangerous.

Joshua was concerned as well and called for word with my friend John. With many hours of journeying to go, we were unsure of the welcome we would receive in Arimathea.

My Master then appointed my brothers, John and Bartholomew, to be sent into Arimathea, as two messengers. They were to find a man carrying water and follow him into the Goodman's house; there the Goodman would prepare a place for our Passover meal. There was much discussion amongst us all about why Joshua had chosen those two to go into Arimathea.

Everyone had a different opinion. Timothy said my Master had chosen them because he loved them more than the rest of us and wanted them to receive God's glory for risking their lives for us. Peter speculated that they were chosen because they were the least loved by Joshua and would be the least missed on the journey!

After allowing sufficient time for our jesting to die down, my Master finally settled our dispute by explaining his reasoning to us. He sent Bartholomew because, being a fisherman in his former life, Joshua knew he would be able to navigate easily through the city. My Master sent John because he wanted him to gain more experience and not be so weak and naive. We looked at one another and nodded agreeably, knowing that he spoke the truth about John needing to acquire more bravery.

Simon scouted out a safe place where we could find rest and led us to a flat area behind a large group of trees that would provide us with cover from the road. It was a beautiful spot near a stream with a breathtaking view of the lights of Arimathea.

It is a curious thing that, although we were in a perfect spot to make camp and it was a warm, comfortable evening, there was a palpable feeling of frustration brewing through all of us.

For weeks on end the Romans had chased us through the mountains. To be sought out by the Romans was a terrible enough fate, but by one's own people? The Sanhedrin and the villagers despised us as well.

It enraged us to think this was due to our conflicting beliefs, and, since most of Arimathea was made up of light skinned Jews, because of our multiple skin colors.

The fact that nearly half of us were dark skinned Jews made us easy targets for contempt and mockery. The Roman soldiers would be much quicker to point us out in the passing crowd, threatening to throw us in jail, almost as if our darker pigment made us more threatening. They always felt threatened.

This was surely the case when one of us expressed any sign of defiance, instilling fear and outrage over every muttered retort. Bartholomew and John explained later that they had experienced a close call earlier when looking for the Goodman's house, but were left unharmed and undisturbed. John confided in me how afraid he was during that moment, but he felt the comfort of the Messiah's presence and stayed brave, a willing messenger.

I still do not understand the basis for such ignorance and prejudice, and I fear I never will. The Torah mentions very little about the color of one's skin. We are all God's children. As we traveled, we saw no apparent differences among Jews in Judea as far as intellect, athleticism, or their nature. Nonetheless, it was an issue that weighed so heavily against us, especially for my Master. There were so many people who seemed to hate him and doubt that he was the Messiah simply because of the color of his skin.

PASSOVER Chapter 6

I was so very grateful when we were navigated safely through Arimathea yesterday, and were finally able to reach the front door of the Goodman's house, cloaked and protected by the camouflage of the dark night.

Tension was in the air from everything that had transpired thus far, and being that it was Passover, we all needed a bit of normalcy from the long journey, camp- outs, and imminent danger lurking at every corner.

But why must they hate him so?

Why would the villagers and rabbis seek to mock and destroy him? Was it because the power that my Master commanded, being a dark-skinned Jew, drove them mad? Was that why some of the rabbis appeared almost as bloodthirsty for his persecution as the Romans?

Upon entering and being received so warmly at the Goodman's house, a great sense of relief and hope seemed to enliven everyone's spirits, washing away our immediate troubles like a cool stream of water on a parched tongue.

As we moved up the stairs, I noticed a visible sign of relief on Peter's face. He had been at his wits end, seeking comfort from our days of endless journeying.

Earlier, Peter had taken my Master aside and complained about the conditions we were forced to endure in the mountains of Judea.

We slept no better than mere rodents, scurrying for food, sometimes going days without nourishment. The scorching sun was insufferable, and I felt the effects of it every step of the way. So did all of the other Disciples. Some like Matthew were bookmen, unused to being worked like horses, at the mercy of the elements. He would have to withhold himself from shouting out loud in complaint, while Peter and I, able fishermen, caught each others' eye trying not to laugh at him.

At times I would have to pause to catch a breath, since the lack of water and steady pace was dizzying. And dear Bartholomew, not having the vigor of some of the more athletic Disciples, began wrapping strips of cloth around his blistered feet and toes as a cushion from the unforgiving soil.

Before long, we all followed suite.

Until I became a Disciple, I never knew what it was like to believe in faith. I didn't know what it meant to fight, and to expand my thinking from the simple life I led before. That outlook was unseasoned; a receptacle of fibrous clay that begged to be formed into its full potential. I was oblivious to anything out of the ordinary. There was no real purpose or intention to my actions; I was simply going through the motions of living. But meeting my Master changed all of that.

I have become a renegade.

My friends at home would not recognize me, and I could never go back to being the person I was before all this occurred. To continue what has been started is my destiny, and my Master's will. I am unsure know where this road will lead, but it does not matter. The gates will be opened to me in the afterlife.

The only matter of importance is spreading the news.

I will shout out his teachings from the highest mountain to the lowest cavern until the day I leave this earth.

As we walked into the small haven where we were to partake in what I now know was to be his very last supper, a sense of joy and community overwhelmed me. I was enjoying the moment, taking in everything around me.

Everything was beautifully arranged.

The room was dimly lit by many candles and smelled of jasmine and spiced meat. The bright, patterned cushions were arranged neatly with exactly thirteen pillows placed around a low standing, oak wood table. The wall was a calming, wood forest green with collected paintings by some of the most well known Judean artists.

The red wine in the pitchers was inviting, and the earth tone, clay plates were ready to be stacked high with tzimmes, matzo, stew and all of the other traditional dishes. We were sorely famished for a real meal after surviving on dried fish and wine for all of those days, I know that I certainly hated the way the fish were preserved with salt, leaving an unpleasant aftertaste in our mouths.

We all bowed our heads in prayer, as is customary, as my Master blessed the food with the hagada prayer.

"All leavened bread and leavening that is in my possession, whether I have observed it or not observed it, whether I have searched it out or not searched it out shall be rendered null and accounted valueless as the dust of the earth."

We began eating the sacred meal as a holy family, bound together by the love of our Messiah. I felt love and gratitude for my fellow Disciples. I appreciated the way we helped one another through the trying times, and the way we all did our best to take care of my Master. This was a collective that I was honored to be a part of. I never would have expected the surprising and horrible news that my Master was about to reveal.

A TRAITOR IS REVEALED Chapter 7

My Master first began to explain the meaning of Passover, and the reason why it is such a special day. He reminded us of what had come to pass when we were freed from the confines of the Egyptian rulers.

During the time of his birth, King Herod had received word from the Magi that my Master, the Messiah, was born as a king of the dark-skinned Judeans. The Magi were joyful and excited, wishing to show their respects to the young Messiah.

The king felt threatened by his presence and began plotting a way to get to my Master. He sent the Magi, blessed with the gift of astrology, to locate my Master by a path found through the stars. He assured them that he only wanted to worship the young King after being informed of his whereabouts.

So the Magi went on to find the young Messiah, bearing gifts of Frankincense and Myrrh. Being warned in a dream not to inform Herod, they followed another path on their way back home.

Herod was furious that he was tricked by the Magi and became obsessed with the thought of killing my Master. He immediately ordered the slaughtering of every first -born male child from a dark-skinned, Jewish family, thinking that was the way he could alleviate the problem!

Fortunately for my Master, his earthly father was warned in a dream by the Father to flee for safety. So my Master, his mother Mary and stepfather, Joseph, escaped and hid from Herod in Egypt, until his death. They fit into their surroundings easily, as their skin tones were chestnut and mahogany colored, like some of the Egyptians.

The bloodshed was an unholy terror, and there were many children dead at the hands of the cruel King. King Herod's murderous attempts stopped when he died, and my Master and his family came back to Nazareth.

As My Master continued to speak of all we were to be thankful for, I could not help but notice the strain in his voice and the melancholy look in his eyes. The Seder meal was a somber and reflective time, but it was as if he were deeply troubled and afflicted. It was a very different demeanor than I had been exposed to before, and I wondered what was on his mind.

As a closing to the sacred meal, we all partook in the unleavened bread and sop. Sop is a thick gravy preparation, made from boiled meat, flour, and spices. It was then stirred and watched for hours until it gained the perfect consistency.

We passed around a container of salt, dropping a pinch of it into our bowls, and then dipped the bread into the mixture. As we were doing this, my Master gravely explained to us that his Father told him that he was going to be betrayed by one who dips their bread into the sop with him that night.

Yes. By one of his blessed and loyal Disciples!

But how could this be?

We were all stunned with shock and disbelief. I looked around the table at my fellow brothers faces, watching for any unusual signs or expressions that might give away their ill intent. I saw nothing but clouded confusion in every man's eyes.

I recounted the days of our journey up until this moment. I had walked and talked with each of these men, and knew them to be good followers. I had shared stories of fishing and my younger school days, overcome fear of death and cruel punishment, and prayed with each and every one of then.

They were my brothers.

I would vouch for all of them.

Peter became so angry upon hearing this that he maniacally drew his sword, calling out the false follower in an outrage. I thought he was going to get into a bloody fight with some of the others, who questioned Peter's love for my Master during the heated banter. I tried to keep quiet so as not to become physically involved. I was unsure of which way to turn or how to help my Master find solace.

Feeling so strongly of our undying love for the Messiah, I addressed the situation.

"No Master, it's impossible! Everyone at this table loves you."

My Master, Joshua, looked me directly in the eye and responded low and urgently.

"Do you call my Father a liar Thomas?" he said.

I felt impotent and nauseated by this revelation. I knew that what the Father observed and ordained would always be true, and although truth gives way to incomparable freedom, there is sometimes a pain that accompanies all that is revealed. None of us wanted to hear that one of our beloved brothers, a traitor revealed, would soon turn on our Master. Certainly not now, when the Messiah was so close to the fulfillment of the prophecy.

It must have been a bittersweet meal for my Master, knowing that he was going to be betrayed by one that he took under his wing and loved so dearly. I was in awe of his love and benevolence. I was also taken aback by the way he accepted the situation without throwing blame or hatred upon the betrayer.

Why would he not point him out, so we could punish and stop the offending Disciple? There were eleven of us, and only one betrayer! It would have been easy to detain the one who strayed! Why would my Master continue speaking to all of us, taking no action against the disciple, in a kind and peaceful manner? Is it possible he did not know the betrayer, knowing only that he would be betrayed?

However, that is the way of my Master, his forgiveness is measureless.

The sacred and comforting atmosphere I had relished in only moments ago had turned into a frenzied, verbal battle; a confusing and terrible argument as to who cared for our Master most, and who was most likely to turn on him in his time of need.

That was when James finally gathered up the courage to ask my Master who would sit next to him in Heaven. We all wanted to know the answer to that burning question, since we had been silently thinking about it for the whole journey. Each Disciple had been doing his best to showcase his undying affection and loyalty.

Then, my Master, Joshua of Nazareth, did the strangest, most mundane thing. In response, he motioned to the servant in the room to hand him a towel and a basin of clean water. The Messiah shed the robes and head coverings he was wearing and wrapped a clean, white towel around his waist.

Kneeling on one knee in the likeness of a common servant, one by one, my Master proceeded to wash our feet.

It was embarrassing and humbling all at the same time. Some of the men, like Peter, even resisted. They believed the task to be beneath my Master. Peter exclaimed that he would never, under any circumstances, let our Master wash his feet. He looked pained at the idea of the Messiah lowering himself. I could not blame him for the way he felt. It was an awkward experience, a King bathing his servants. We wondered why my Master would do such a thing!

My master told Peter "If you do not wash your feet, you will not have any part of me."

Peter looked down for a moment, thoughtfully. His eyes grew misty with tears of love. After a moment, he responded that in that case, my Master should wash his head, his hands, and every other part of his body. My Master assured him that he only needed to obey his order and cleanse his feet to be washed of his sins and be part of the Messiah.

He also said that there were some of us who would never be clean.

I felt a sinking of my stomach as I looked around, knowing that he spoke of the traitor amongst us. My Master then explained that he used the foot bathing as a metaphor. He wanted to embed the image of serving others into our minds, so that we might remember to always serve the Father, and serve those around us when he was no longer there to guide us.

His love for us was that strong.

My Master then blessed a cup of red wine and drunk from it. He said that the wine represented the blood that he was going to shed for our sins, and that the next time he tasted of it, he would be next to his Father in his kingdom.

After the prayer he passed the cup around the table, and each of us somberly took a sip from the goblet. He then blessed a piece of bread, telling us that this symbolized his human body, broken and sacrificed for us. We all ate of the bread in silence, thinking about the words he spoke to us.

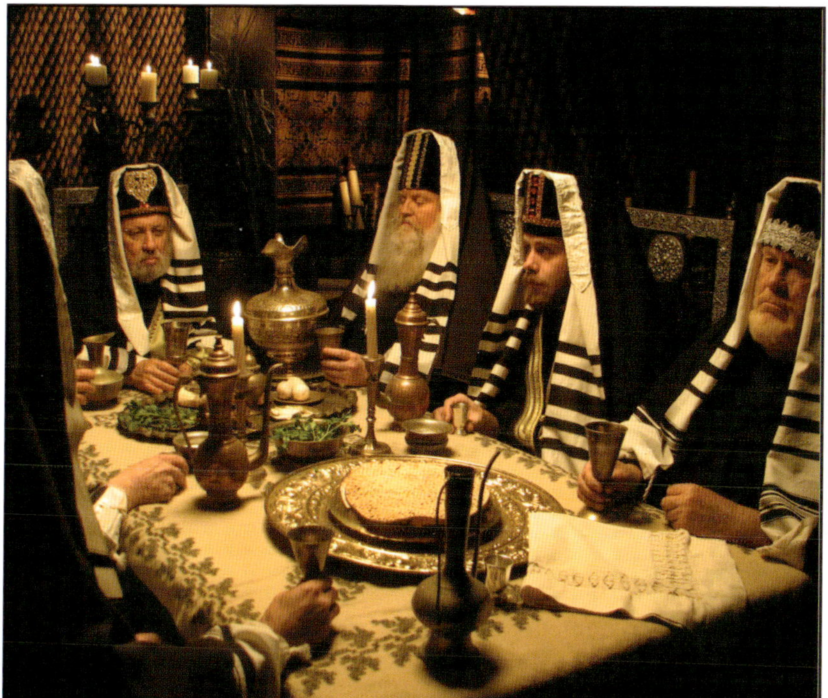

DANGER! Chapter 8

After this was finished, we were almost discovered by the Roman soldiers. Village informants tipped off the Sanhedrin, the Jewish judicial council of Rabbis, at Lishkat Ha-gazith and they sent for us, breaking down the door to the Goodman's house and harassing him and his family! The whole house shook when Horatius and the other guards searched the bottom floor. We could hear them shouting at the Goodman and his family.

"Have you seen a black Jew?" Horatius exclaimed, "Under penalty of death you had better speak the truth!"

The Goodman was a very brave man and did not reveal my Master's identity, even when his life was at stake. His daughter, Sarah, was so afraid she couldn't help but scream out loud, defending her father's innocence. But still the Goodman swore that he had seen no dark-skinned Nazareen, and if he did, that he would promise to seek him out.

The Centurion guard was not pleased with the Goodman's answers, and caused a commotion by smashing a Jewish heirloom onto the Passover table, while the other soldiers tore down the curtains in the dining room in an attempt to further intimidate the brave Goodman.

Still, he did not flinch in the face of danger, and he will surely be rewarded for his dauntlessness!

We fled as soon as the last horses' hooves were but an echo in the distance, and I didn't have much time to ponder over what the next day might bring, let alone who the traitor was in our midst. The most painful revelation of all was that our Messiah also revealed that every last one of us would soon fall away from him, and Peter, who loved him most fiercely, would deny our Master three times before the cock crowed!

Once again, this drew looks of concern and dismay from us all.

We all knew that Peter loved my Master both passionately and urgently. He made it a point to protect my Master at all times, no matter what we were up against! Peter was the Messiah's dearest friend here on this earth and would give his life to save my Master. This did not make any sense!

Later, John told me that he overheard the Messiah speaking to the deceiver. He said our Master was so forgiving and loving he even blessed the back stabber and kissed him good-bye.

He communicated the terrible news to me that night, at our final camping site, beneath the stars. I realized that we had become so close throughout this passage; he was a true friend. I suppose dangerous experiences and enlightenment brings people together in a way that only growth and truth can.

He spoke of the incident with a sullen and cold look on his face, more of a grown man than I'd ever seen him. It seems life had matured him.

He told me that my Master had confirmed that it was our beloved Judas that would lead the enemy to our King, and, earlier, that John had tried to stop him by almost slicing his throat before he ran off into the night. He came up softly behind Judas with the element of surprise and proceeded to threaten him.

"Breathe a sound Traitor!" John whispered, as he wrapped his arm around Judas' neck.

He continued to hold the vise-like grip, as Judas made a meek and frightful noise. The cold steel of John's blade paralyzed him with fear.

"Even in betrayal, he is glorious. If it were not for him, I would have gladly opened your throat!" he said.

John unsheathed his sword to show me that there was a bit of dried blood crusted onto the sharp metal. He had been serious about sparing Judas only because of the Messiah. He silently finished buffing his sword with a soft, dry cloth while I looked on, thoughtfully. As proud as I was of John finally being able to stand up for my Master, I was saddened more deeply than you can imagine that my brother would be brought to such a low point.

Judas ran off into the night, fearful for his life after John confronted him. I can only imagine where he could have taken refuge. The streets of Gethsemane were dangerous for us. The townspeople had no idea that Judas had betrayed his Master. They certainly would not care to hear about it if they caught and surrounded him. All they wanted was blood! They sought out anyone who was a self-proclaimed "Lover of Black Jews," wanting them to be jailed or worse, beaten or tortured.

The Temple Precincts would not be easy to get to on this night. There were Roman soldiers everywhere, knocking down the doors of every dark-skinned Jewish household, wrecking their furniture and rattling nerves.

It was an outrage! Did having a darker pigment constitute such questioning and violence? Also, simply because my Master was a Black Jew, did that automatically mean everyone that looked like him believed his words, and would risk their lives to conceal him? Certainly not!

But the Centurions thought little about such details. All they wanted was to discover my Master, and were willing to wreck and ravage every Black household to get to their goal!

I pray for the souls of the Romans and of the Sanhedrin.

The situation was becoming worse by the hour. Some guards had even lit fires around the town, so that billowing smoke and the smell of coal and ash was everywhere. It was a challenge to navigate through the frenzied crowds, and it must have been difficult for Judas to conceal himself.

But there was one person, (it was rumored,) Judas made it a point to seek out that night, a person that he was obsessed with. There were many things I have doubted but of this I was almost certain.

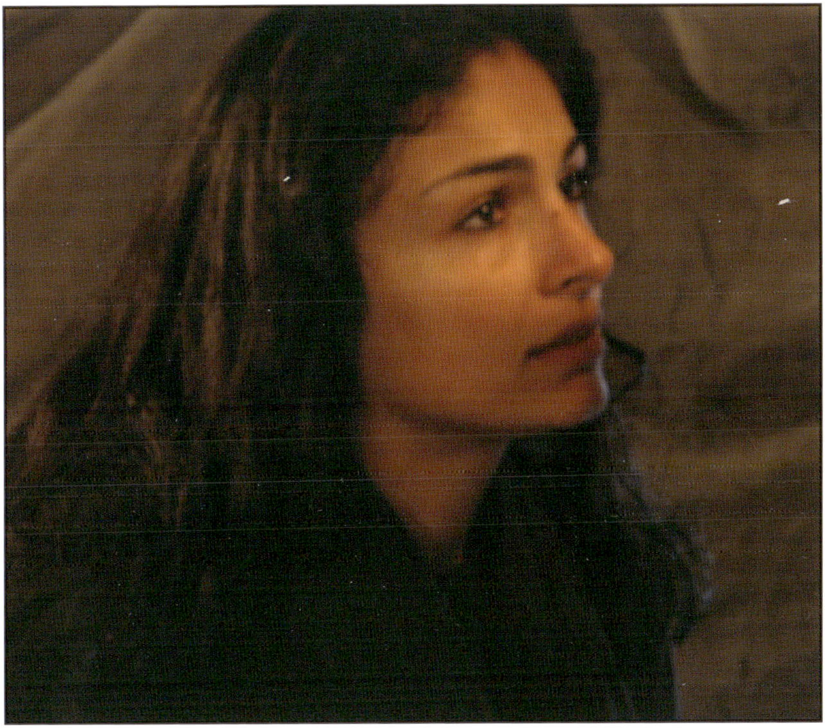

AN UNLIKELY FRIENDSHIP Chapter 9

Mary Magdalene was a maiden of the night. A woman in her thirties who abandoned the only family that she had, she walked the streets in search of a shiny coin and promise of a new tomorrow, a wandering hermit. She was a striking and dusky beauty. The lady was fair of skin with chestnut tresses, and smoldering eyes that beckoned one to come hither.

She knew the entire circle of well to do, single men in the surrounding towns, as well as those that had wives. It didn't matter what their story was, as long as they had an endless supply of silver and a jug of wine to last through the nights of pleasure. Her promise was one of complete satisfaction for a man's deepest worldly desires, and the woman was excellent at delivering just that.

When I first saw Mary Magdalene, I thought her to be almost unreal. She wore the same plain cotton robes as the other women, with the same head scarves and simple sandals.

But there was something about her that was undoubtedly enticing.

In broad daylight, walking along the cobblestone, she would playfully let the coarse material covering her face slide to one side and off of her forehead. The silky hairs that fell to her waistline shone brightly in the sunlight. As she turned, the outline of her voluptuous bosom was highlighted against the thin, wheat- colored sack clothes. Her walk was one of importance and sensuality, she knew she was not an innocent little girl, nor did she care to be thought of as one.

The strangest thing was that my Master, Joshua, had a deep affinity for Miss Magdalene. He happened upon her on the street one day when he was schooling a group of young men on their faith. They had all gathered round to hear what the Messiah had to say, enthralled to be in the presence of someone so noteworthy.

Some of the teenage boys brought a barrel of ripe, red and yellow oranges, and offered the delectable fruits to my Master and the rest to us Disciples.

I peeled one of them eagerly, biting into the bright, fleshy wedges, and let the sweet juices dribble down my chin, smiling.

The fruit tasted delicious, as we had become so accustomed to our bland, dried portions.

There was one tiny boy dressed in rags, about the age of 6, who was excited and earnest to learn more about my Master and his teachings. The boy did not look like he had any parents, or, if he did, then they were quite destitute, letting him run rampant in the streets. His sandals were worn through with holes, and there was dirt on his face and matted hair.

He came and sat by the Messiah's feet so that he could listen to my Master's storytelling, and see the expressions on his face as he spoke of his love for mankind, no matter how big or how small, either rich or poor. My Master picked the boy up and sat him on his lap while he continued his speech, and the little one grinned from ear to ear, ecstatic.

Suddenly, there was a great crash in the distance, and the breaking of a window angrily resounded a few paces away from where my Master was teaching. We all looked up to see what was going on. A large, roaring crowd of villagers were pointing fingers and yelling out obscenities uncontrollably! But what could have infuriated the crowd in such a way? Many people ran from their homes to watch and join in on the rioting.

"Look Master", said the young boy. "They are trying to hurt her!"

The silhouette of a man and indecently clad woman could be seen through the broken window, and the woman was hurrying to dress herself in her robes while some people jabbed long sticks through the opening and called her names.

The man slipped out through the side wooden gate, but no one paid him any attention. His actions did not seem to matter to anyone. They were all focused intently on the lady.

"Evil witch!" said one woman

"Jezebel – you're not fit to live another day!" screamed out another.

The woman, spooked, back up from the window, narrowly escaping a flamed torch that was thrown her way. We all gasped in alarm. This was getting out of hand! The woman could be seriously injured or worse, killed!

The house burst into flames, and the crowd cheered. Luckily the woman found a hidden back door to aid in her escape, and when she reached the alleyway, started running for her life. I breathed a sigh of relief, glad that the raven-haired lady had found a way to sneak around the dangerous crowds. She had come very close to being in a terrible situation.

However, just as she rounded the bend of the alleyway, she stumbled over some loose debris, tumbling to the ground, and the sound of her sandal soles resounded loudly on the hollow turf!

One man saw her and yelled to the rest of the crowd to follow her.

"Let's get the sinner! "

"There she goes! "

"Let's stone the devil's helper!"

The villagers ran after the woman, grabbing loose rocks from the worn cobblestone roads and any other large, oblong pieces of rubbish that they could find. Meanwhile, my Master gently set the boy down and followed the crowd, walking at a brisk pace. I followed him with a worrisome expression on my face.

Would we be too late?

Why would they want to stone the beautiful woman?

Like a mouse trapped in a corner by a hissing feline, the lovely woman was caught in a terrible bind. On one end the villagers were gathered forty people strong with stones in hand, glaring ominously; while on the other side, stood a walnut tree near a short ledge, overlooking the bank a river bank while gushing waters streamed greedily below. What would she choose?

Surely she would not jump into the river?

The woman clung to the branch of the tree, staring fatefully at the approaching crowd. She had a calm look on her face, despite the fact that she may have very well been facing her death. She even broke into bitter, almost maniacal laughter as they continued to harass and approach her. It wasn't looking well for her, and my Master motioned us to approach the righteous demonstrators.

Suddenly, my Master parted the group.

He asked the crowd why they wished to stone the woman. They told the Messiah that she was an unmarried woman that was discovered committing pre-marital relations with a well to do businessman in the town.

She had a reputation that preceded her, and had been disturbing marriages and selling her womanly comfort for years.

She preyed on young men and high classed gentlemen, skulking the alleys and streets for a living. This was the moment they had all been waiting for. The bottom feeder was finally caught in the act of adultery.

One villager yelled out that they should all raise their sticks and stones, and when he had finished counting thrice, then that was the moment to let the woman have what was coming to her! Then my Master did a wondrous thing.

He came and stood right in front of the woman!

There was no way for the villagers to harm the woman without first attacking my Master. The crowd was infuriated. They told him to get out of the way, and let them continue their business.

"Can't you see this woman is poisonous?" one said.

"We are only doing this for the greater good!" chimed in another.

The woman looked confused, but very grateful to whoever her mysterious savior was. My Master then addressed the crowd, taking a moment to survey each and every face. He announced to the people that whoever was without sin should throw the first stone. One heavyset man grew very impatient with my Master.

"Your words mean nothing to me!" he exclaimed. "Why do you defend her? She is unworthy of having her pitiful life spared!"

Solemnly, slowly, the Messiah repeated the same words. Whoever is without sin, please cast the first stone. A surge of guilt seemed to rise up from the people, and some looked down at their feet. Others, confused, turned to the person next to them, looking for an answer or prompt.

Then the most amazing thing happened.

The angry women lowered their pointed sticks from above their heads, and mumbled amongst themselves. Some sat on the ground, deep in thought. Then, one by one, the stones began to drop with a clank on the ground, and the crowd dispersed, until only the heavyset man and a handful of others were left.

My Master then came and placed his hands on the heavyset man's shoulder. He quietly spoke into the man's ear words that I could only speculate upon, attempting to alleviate tension between the villager and the poor woman. The man shook his head in response and looked at the woman.

Then, he wrapped his arms around the Messiah, and like a newborn baby, began to cry out loud!

John, Bartholomew and I reassuringly looked to one another, as we were all relieved that there was to be no stoning. We motioned for the other perplexed villagers to go about with their day and leave the area, while my Master, after comforting the man, gently approached the woman.

"What is your name, child of Jehovah?" he asked kindly.

My Master's eyes showed brightly, filled with empathy and compassion. The woman paused for a moment, still clinging to the branch, as if without it, she might topple to the ground. She was silent for a moment, and finally spoke in a pleasant, low tone.

"My name is Mary, Mary of Magdalene," she said. "I will be forever grateful to you for helping spare my life".

She peered at him wonderingly, and then turned her attention to the rest of us, his loyal followers. Then, an expression of understanding passed over her face. Mary looked straight at the Messiah and asked my Master if he was the one that the townspeople had been talking about, the prophet who claimed to be the Son of God.

My Master smiled and replied that indeed he was the Son of the Father, but was unsure if he was the man the people had been gossiping about. Trivial talk and pettiness would not hold the attention of my Master.

She nodded in response.

As befitting his place, my Master took the opportunity to use Mary Magdalene's inquiry as a lesson. He explained to her that gossip was ungodly and unfitting for a humble servant seeking only to bring light unto the world, and that such chatter brought little good to anyone who took part in it.

This cracked a smile from the remarkably beautiful woman, who had probably endured the repercussions of gossip and jealousy for much of her life. Having said this, my Master took her hand and clasped it in his own. Although I had not realized it at that moment, this marked the beginning of an unlikely friendship for my Master and Mary of Magdalene.

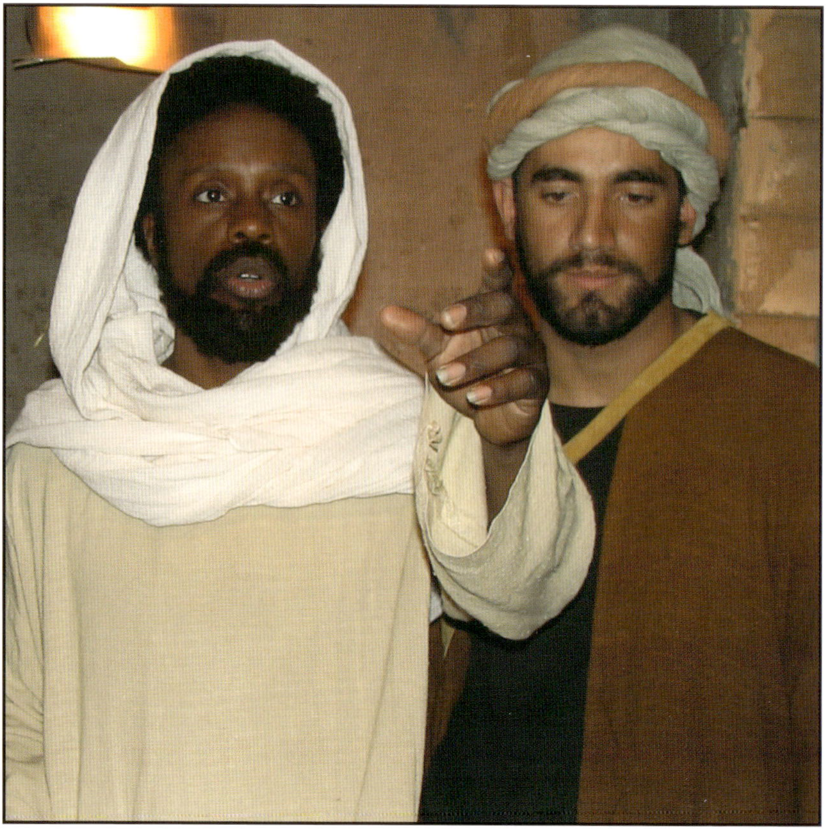

SATAN BEGONE Chapter 10

They walked and talked by themselves for hours, and my Master knelt and prayed for Mary that her spirit would be freed of any and all demons possessing her. The woman was visibly moved by the Messiah and had found solace in his gentle character.

She asked him for forgiveness of the sins that she had committed, and the occupation she had chosen to pursue. My Master placed his hands on her head in a gesture of healing. The woman closed her eyes to receive her blessing, and then started to gasp, turning from side to side and shaking from head to toe! This continued for some time. Suddenly, she became still, and immediately following that, let out a number of high-pitched screams that sounded agonizing! We all jumped, not knowing what to do.

John looked to me worryingly.

My Master was exorcising the demons from her body!

Then the woman's eyes opened and rolled backwards, and she started to break out into a deep sweat. I saw the shadows being pulled out of the woman's body, one by one. It was terrible and mesmerizing all at the same time. The dark spirits were all different shapes and sizes. Some had a red haze that floated around them, like a bloody halo encircling their engorged outlines.

"Satan begone!" the Messiah shouted.

Others were green tinged and whirled about, with sounds like the hissing winds marking their exits. There was one especially difficult demon that fought my Master for quite some time, but the Messiah prevailed, and the monster was cast out, echoing throughout the town with its baleful moan! I counted seven shadows being pulled from the woman's body altogether.

This was almost more that I could take! We had followed my Master for years, but this was by far the most dramatic healing that any of us had seen. All of the villagers came back outside and witnessed the exorcism, whispering frantically among them.

Then finally the woman breathed a sigh of relief, feeling the waves of the devil's playmates being washed away from her mortal body for eternity. We all cheered! This was an astounding miracle performed by my Master! It was a breathtaking sight, the pair of them.

Right then and there Mary Magdalene swore to be one of my Master's followers, just as we twelve Disciples were, preaching his words to all.

The others and I looked skeptically at one another. This had never happened before, the rest of us were all men! The Messiah had hand picked each and every one of us to be his appointed soldiers. Mary Magdalene, on the other hand, volunteered her own soul, and she was a woman at that!

Could a woman truly be a chosen Disciple?

It was hard to believe that Mary Magdalene found such favor with the Messiah, but my Master was highly pleased with her proclamation. None of us had ever seen our Master like this before; he was carefree and light of heart. Mary Magdalene brought joy and comfort to his soul in a way that only a woman's presence could. To have traveled among male Disciples for all of this time, it was intriguing to see my Master behave in such a way. Some of the Disciples whispered loudly amongst themselves as my Master and Mary Magdalene walked together, no better than a group of gossiping wives.

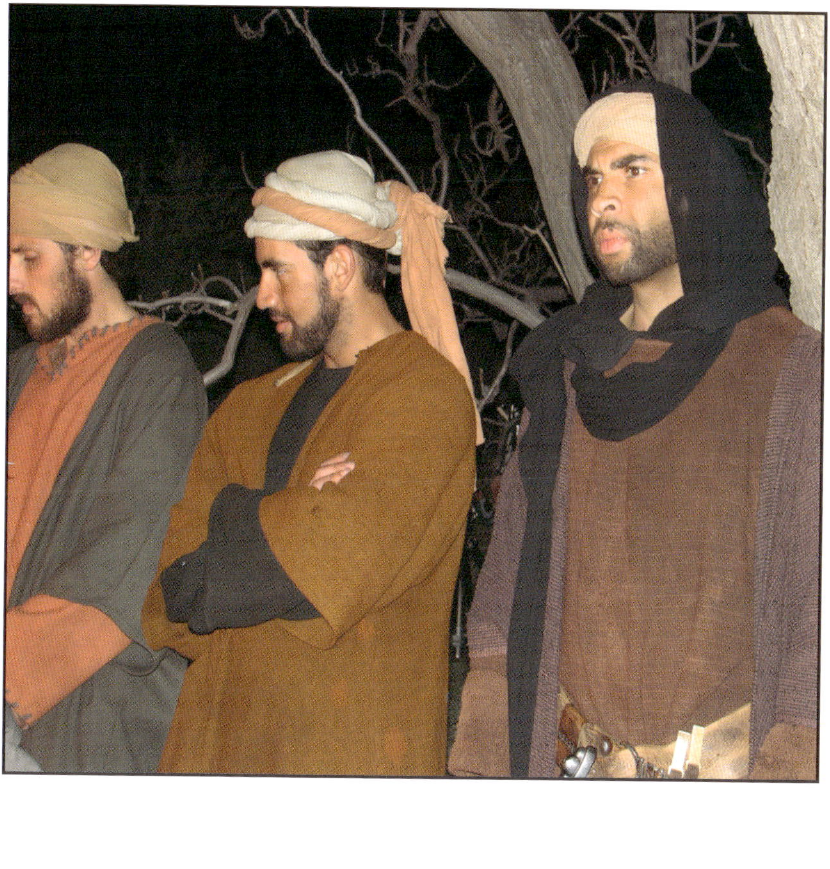

THE START OF TEMPTATION Chapter 11

But as all this was going on, I noticed Judas becoming affected in a very strange manner. Like the rest of the Disciples, as all men, he was instantly struck by Mary Magdalene's pleasing figure and arresting looks.

But Judas took it much further.

He actually seemed bewitched by the female and couldn't take his eyes off of her, following Mary Magdalene and my Master as they walked and talked. He lived for her alluring smile and contagious laughter. He often sat next to her during my Master's lessons, and made it a point to converse with her during times of fellowship. This was the start of Judas' earthly temptation, appearing in the likeness of a beautiful woman.

My Master's strong connection with the woman was obvious to all, and Judas grew more and more envious of their closeness. Judas ultimately worshipped the ground that Mary Magdalene walked on, and was always there to offer a cool drink from a pitcher of water whenever she appeared for lessons, or a blanket to rest on as shelter from the hot sands.

But no matter what Judas did to show Mary Magdalene how much he adored her, she was at most, obligingly attentive. He was a distraction from the truth to her. Her thoughts and conversations were saved only for my Master, and from the looks of it, she absorbed every word he uttered.

And although considered by society as an unclean, heathenish female, Mary Magdalene was undeniably intelligent.

The woman was ingeniously gifted with a skillful mind, remembering my Master's stories word for word. Most of us would take notes on my Master's teachings to better remember the lessons, but she could recall countless events, stored in her memory, on a moments notice. She would repeat his passages passionately, putting the rest of us Disciples to shame when it came to dissecting the parables. The men, especially Peter, were guarded and competitive, not wanting to be outdone by her.

She dived into many debates with Matthew and Peter regarding the scriptures. Those two men loved to sit for hours and pour over the Torah, comparing traditional values to the words of my Master. She spoke freely, touching on every subject as boldly as if she had been studying my Master's words for years!

None of us had ever witnessed anything like it. Her gift was undeniable.

The other factor, besides her being a self appointed female Disciple, was that Mary Magdalene came and went as she pleased. She never apologized or abandoned her craft or livelihood, unlike the rest of us brothers.

For example, my days of fishing were long gone, as were the other Disciple's professions. Our sole occupation was to serve and protect the Messiah. Her approach was radical and even upsetting to some. To some of us, if not all, it was presumptuous and sinful of her to comprehend the teachings of my Master but continue to live her life as if she weren't enlightened.

Somehow, Mary Magdalene always found her way back to my Master, warmly welcoming us all into Arimathea or another of the surrounding towns. When the crowds would gather and beg for deliverance, I would observe her curled up against a large rock, hands clasped together, head alert.

No matter how many hundreds of people came that day, or how many healings my Master performed, there she would wait, a perfect pupil. Secretly, I respected Mary Magdalene and her devotion to my Master. She possessed an endurance that put our own schooling efforts, in effect for years, to shame. It was inspiring.

However, it made some of my fellow brothers uncomfortable.

Peter was very vocal about his wariness for Mary Magdalene. He loved my Master protectively, and always assessed the girl competitively. He was of the opinion that a woman should be at home with her family, not out wandering the streets with my Master. But in the presence of the Messiah, he was cordial, not wanting to challenge my Master's judgment too severely and upset him.

When he spoke of her, it was with a more subtle approach. He told my Master that he was worried about him. Mary Magdalene was from a harsh background, running wild in the streets and run down inns. He pondered aloud the possibility of Mary Magdalene influencing the Messiah and the other Disciples, seducing them with her feminine wiles and suggestive appearance. Although he allowed Peter to voice his thoughts, my Master had only good things to say about her. And so, Mary of Magdalene became a permanent fixture in our circle.

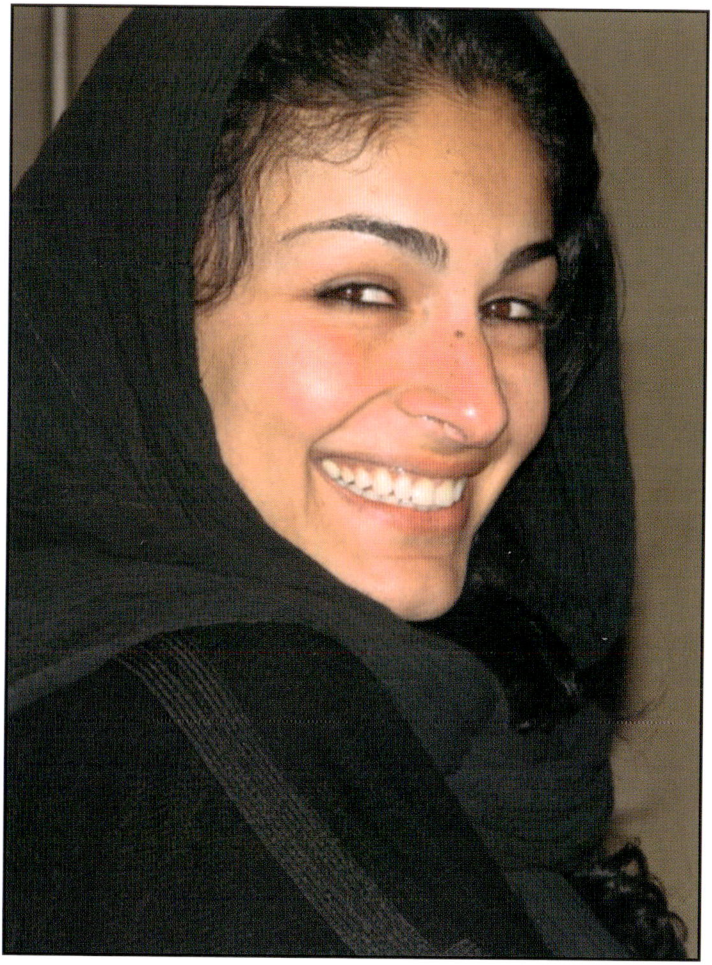

DELIRIUM Chapter 12

As the weeks went on, Judas' fascination with Mary Magdalene grew all the more. It was unhealthy and ungodly to lust so openly for a woman. However, he didn't seem to realize the hold that she had on him. He was a tormented soul, envisioning sinful encounters by day and writing undelivered letters of devotion by the fire at night.

After some time, Judas' admiration for Mary Magdalene turned sour. He not only begrudged my Master, Joshua of Nazareth, for holding all of her attention, but brooded over Mary Magdalene's rejection.

He was certain that, if not for my Master's position, Mary Magdalene would be his. She would be able to see Judas for the leader that he certainly was, not just a mere Disciple. Many ill thoughts began to form in his mind.

He pictured himself free of my Master, taking Mary Magdalene home to be his wife. He also pictured a mysterious meeting with her on the dark streets, accompanying her to a local tavern for wine and dancing. After they were finished, she would embrace his kisses and they would lie together at last.

This was the beginning of the end, the cause of destruction for my traitorous brother, I think. He yearned for the woman so desperately that it took a large toll on his sanity. His eyes became lost and unfocused at times while we traveled and I could tell that he was thinking of her, smitten. It was troubling to witness. The devil preyed on Judas' soul through the likeness of a woman. He became trapped in a delirium, one of his own making.

Many times, my Master has told us that no man should look lustfully upon a woman that is not his wife, and to think such a thought is the same as committing the act of adultery itself! I was astounded when I first heard this, but it made sense to me after a while. We must all do our best to think pure thoughts, so that our bodies will be in accordance with our minds. My Master's ways are challenging and meant only for those who vow of complete surrender is true, sacred, and humble.

Peter saved most of his commentary regarding Mary Magdalene's position for the rest of us. He stirred up some of my brothers, who shared a similar opinion. I myself did not understand the need for such outrage. Were they against Mary Magdalene just because she was a woman? She had more than proven her love for the words and teachings of the Messiah!

After all, we are the Father's children. We all wanted to spread my Master's love around the world, and that's all that should have mattered, at least in my eyes, and in the eyes of my Master.

If only the others felt the same way.

Despite the varied tension amongst all of us, it was clear that the Messiah doted on Mary Magdalene, and none could come between the God-blessed bonds that they shared. But as the days and weeks went on, apparently unchanged between my Master and Mary Magdalene, Judas' malcontented nature consumed him.

Judas couldn't figure out why Mary Magdalene didn't respond to his polite gestures and light flirtations. It was obvious to all that he thought her to be the most beautiful woman to walk the earth. I even observed him sketching her image during the last traces of dusk, penning words of admiration along the bottom of the parchment. John giggled watching his actions as well, and poked me lightly in the ribcage.

After he finished his illustration, he gazed longingly at the picture. And later, he tucked the roll of papyrus into his pocket, clutching it protectively as he fell asleep.

I imagine he likely dreamt of her that night.

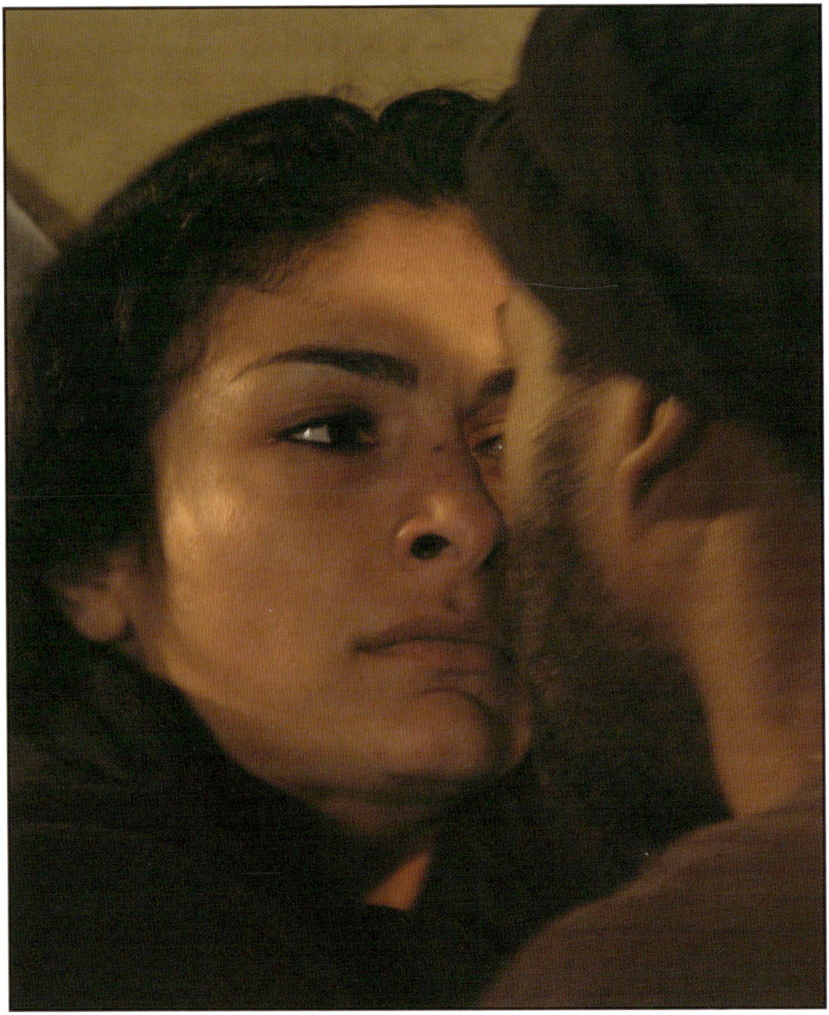

IT HAS BEGUN Chapter 13

It was with very little surprise that we received whispers amongst the villagers, later, that Judas had visited Mary Magdalene on his way to the Temple Precincts that night.

Mary Magdalene took station in Gethsemane, watching out for my Master as she always did when he made his way into town, since his actions were always relayed to her through reliable sources. Supposedly Mary Magdalene took refuge in small, inconspicuous quarters, as the news of the Messiah's danger was making Mary Magdalene fear for my Master's life.

Knowing Mary, she'd have wanted to see and speak to him, to aid him by comforting and listening to his thoughts. Above all, she would have wanted to get to my Master before he was discovered and taken from this earth, as proclaimed by the Father. She would have known that his time was nearing.

Later, Judas was spotted running toward the Temple Precincts in Gethsemane, in the thick of the uproarious crowd. It was a walking nightmare: people shouting and screaming at the top of their lungs, fires blazing along the outskirts of the town and entrances, and violent fights breaking out among the villagers.

I can almost hear the villager's cries:
"Kill the Black Jew!"

"They are dirtier than pigs!"

Yes. No King of our people could look like that!"

"He lies! He will pay for blaspheming the Torah!"

The crowds were uncontrollable, fueled by a hateful prejudice. To think this was all because of the Centurions and the Rabbis! They kept feeding lies to the people about my Master, and persecuting him for something he and many others had been born with, a darker skin color! It was an atrocity.

In passing, I overheard many villagers gossiping, saying that Mary Magdalene had seen Judas running in the crowd, and invited him in to take shelter. She was alarmed that he was out in full view during such a dangerous time. We had all become so infamous that he was likely to be recognized. If that were to happen, there's no telling what the people would have done to Judas!

Perhaps someone would have cornered him and beaten him. Or, he could have been viciously stoned by a group of dark skinned Nazareen haters. Even if a villager was to have summoned the Romans to capture him, the crowd was so enraged that they would have surely placed their own punishment on his head before they delivered him!

Yes, Judas was in a very dangerous place at the time.

This must have been what ran through Mary Magdalene's mind when she picked him out in the crowd. But little did she know at the time that he was on the way to betray my Master! She was entirely unaware of the dastardly deed he was about to commit. Oh Judas, you have chosen your fate now. My traitorous brother will burn below, for all eternity!

Or did she figure it out?

Maybe Mary Magdalene, being the shrewd thinker and negotiator that she was, figured out Judas' evil plans! She knew that he was headed in the direction of the rabbis. Perhaps she guessed his intentions? After all, Judas was in a very suspicious position.

She must have realized that it was a time of grave danger for my Master there in Gethsemane, inappropriate for running errands or for the re-stocking of supplies. Yes, I do believe Mary Magdalene would have figured out Judas' position! An intelligent woman, she would have seen the guilt written all over his face, and known that the unraveling of our Master's teachings had begun.

I believe that, if aware, Mary Magdalene would have indeed tried to stop Judas from reaching his goal of revealing my Master. Not a very large woman, she would hardly have been able to detain the man physically. He would have quickly knocked her to the floor, and being in such a deranged mindset, could have hurt her very badly.

No, Mary Magdalene would have had to use other tactics.

And although she was hardly interested in Judas' advances, Mary Magdalene was certainly aware of them. She had been in the profession of pleasing and promiscuity for the better part of her life. She knew when a man was interested in pursuing her. She knew what great lengths a man like that would go to in order to get what he wanted.

Even in the act of betrayal.

In the past, she did her best to ignore his lewd suggestions, whispered in passing, too low for my Master's ears to hear. The only reason that she had not slapped him boldly across the cheek was out of love of the Messiah, since Judas was one of his beloved, chosen Disciples. Judas would trail behind the rest of us and wait for her, raising his voice to her at times, demanding to know what she saw in the Messiah that he himself did not possess.

She told him that she saw truth in my Master.

My Master was a man of serenity and goodwill. However, Judas the Zealot did not agree with the Messiah's peace-making ways. Mary Magdalene admired my Master for preaching hope and faith. Trying to win favor by mocking the Messiah, Judas would comment that my Master was incapable of protecting a real woman, and that his ways were too passive.

He urged her to follow him, to be with him, and love him in the way she loved my Master. Sometimes he got so worked up that he would press her against the cobblestone walls in a sensual way when the rest of us were too far off to notice. She would push his hungry hands away from her curvaceous figure in disgust.

Yes. Mary would have been well aware that the most effective way to detain vile Judas was not to block his way. She would have had to indulge him in a feast he had never tasted before. She would have had to sacrifice her body in the name of the Messiah!

Also, knowing Judas' passion for Mary Magdalene, if he had the opportunity to lie with her he would certainly take his time in doing so, under any circumstances. When it came to her, Judas was animalistic. He would have no conscious or thought of consequence, for he desired the woman too greatly.

Even on the eve of my Master's death!

Yes, Judas would have let her tease him until he could be led on no further, and then taken her body with a voracity that only a man that had been denied a woman could. Although ineffective in fully stopping Judas from the betrayal, Mary Magdalene would have hoped to at least postpone him for a short while.

Perhaps.... But ah, this is all but speculation. Only the Father knows what truly happened, and only He can pass judgment as he sees fit, in heaven.

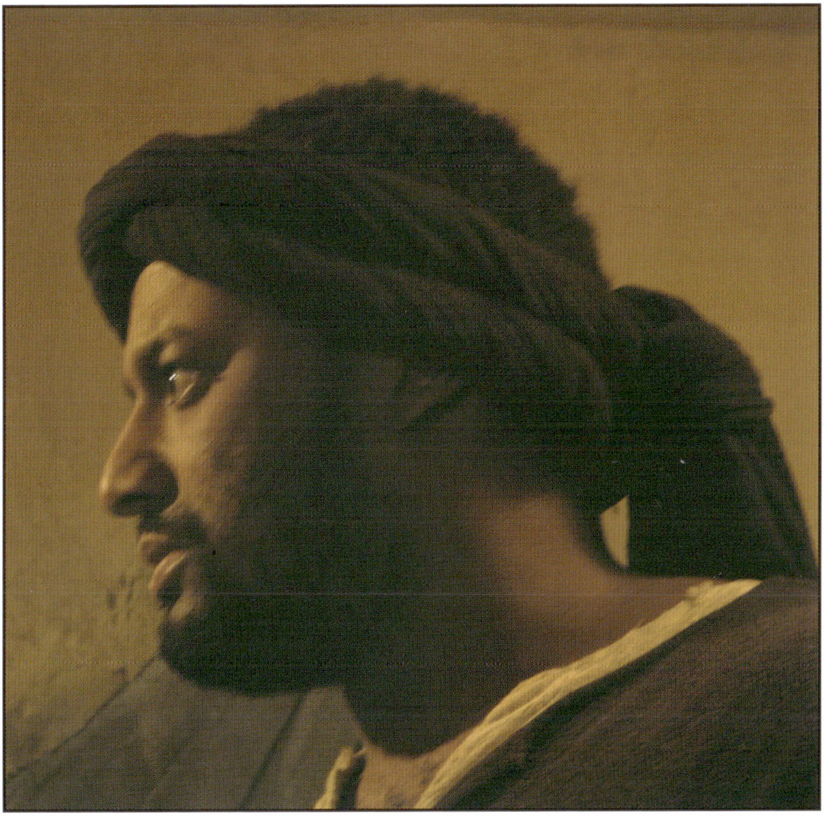

THE DREAM Chapter 14

Reflecting on the choices Judas has made, it's hard for me not to all but despise the man I've come to know as a friend and sacred confidante.

He is a liar and conniver of the worst kind. Like a loved and nurtured dog that ungratefully turned and bit his Master, Judas is a vicious beast in disguise.

He is a like Lucifer!

But he believes differently. On many nights, Judas talked about how he was going to aid in the fulfillment of the prophecy. I must admit that I didn't think much of his confessions; we all wanted to assist my Master.

We all loved him.

But Judas would insist that he had a very special blessing to bestow upon my Master, one that only he had the courage to complete. He also mentioned recurring visions he had experienced along our travels.

An astonishing figure in amber and gold robes, resembling an angel, was visiting him during his night dreams. The angel would speak to Judas in foreign tongues, and the messengers' words were like a symphony of characters flowing effortlessly from his mouth. The delightful angel was sent to help guide Judas toward his purpose.

It was a purpose only known to Judas himself.

The heavenly creature also assured him that his duties were an essential part of the Father's sacred plans. To me, the dreams were perhaps an outlet for his coping during the difficult journey; a gift from the Father, such as Peter's sense of humor or John's penmanship. I must admit, after seeing how affected he was by Mary Magdalene, I had all but tuned Judas' confessions out, tiring of hearing him speak so redundantly.

Had I taken the time to listen further, I would have been able to see how delusional my untrustworthy brother, Judas, has become. I can barely begin to comprehend it, or shed light onto the "when's" and "why's" he has chosen to stray from the fold. However, Judas of Iscariot will face his demons in the afterlife and pay for all that's been committed.

My Master talks freely about the Father's kingdom. We all know that anyone who is lukewarm in their faith will be held in contempt by the Father and be spit from His mouth. There is only pain in suffering in the dark place where Judas will live.

This I do know.

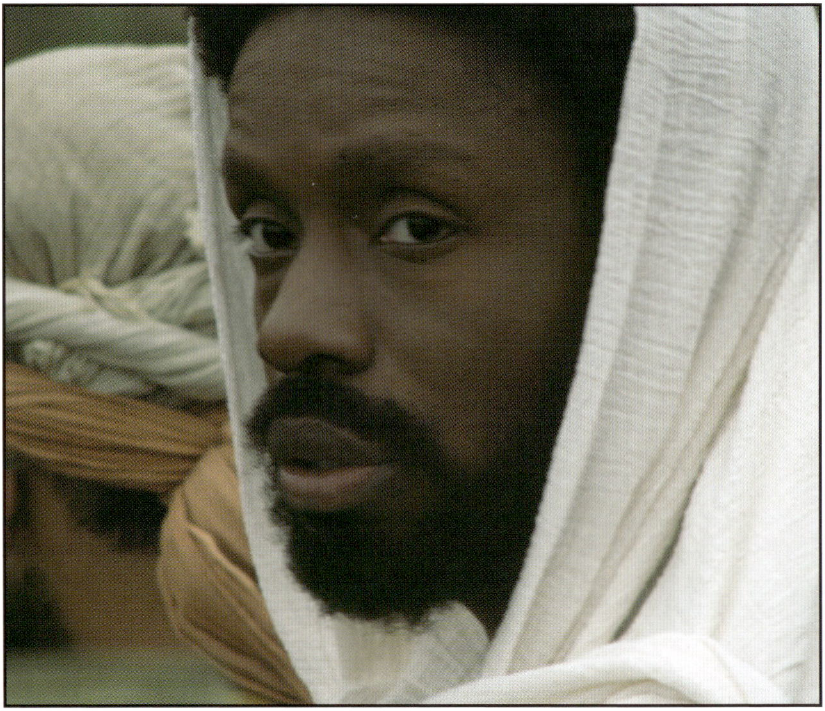

WHAT LIES AHEAD? Chapter 15

We continued on, our path lit by moonlight. The air was crisp and no sounds could be heard save for the chirping of the crickets and Simon and Bartholomew humming a lovely passage.

Their voices blended together so harmoniously, with Bartholomew taking the rich baritone notes while Simon the clear, silken, tenor line. The rest of us, not vocally talented, kept the 4/4 timing with a light snap of our fingers. There is something about music and song that, during times of trouble, is an expression that can help ease the heart.

And although we were nestled in the snugness of tranquil surroundings along the outskirts of Gethsemane, with much talking amongst us, we were all undeniably afraid. Even my Master, I am sure of it. But still, he sought to soothe our spirits and bring light to the dark. The future seemed so bleak, waiting for them to come for my Master and we were uncertain of what lay ahead.

We were all thinking in circles, speculating as to what it would be like. Would it be in here, on the path to Gethsemane, or when we reached the town's border? Would a Nazareen- hating villager, innocently passing by, discover and then reveal us to the Romans? Or, would my Master be so weary of running from his fate that he would surrender himself to the Temple and the Sanhedrin at his own will?

Would they capture us as well and, out of spite, slay us all?

Just contemplating what could be was enough to make my intensity rise to great heights. Even Peter's joking could not crack a smile from any of us, although we pretended to be amused, for our Master's sake.

Along the road to Gethsemane, likening his sacrifice to that of a leaf of wheat falling to the ground, my Master explained to us the natural progression of death, as to bring forth the new fruits of life. I must admit, I was unsure of the point he was trying to make, but attentive nonetheless.

As we progressed into the night, the strain began to show on my Master's face and John and I looked at each other worriedly, unable to shake the feeling of impending danger. How could we reassure our Master of our love and his safety? What words could ease the promise of imminent capture?

Not knowing what to say, I walked on silently.

He stopped at a clearing to pray and we all welcomed the rest. The mental exhaustion was comparable to that of our legs and feet, and, although my body was relaxed, my nerves were on edge. Some of us were summoned to watch over my Master as he came to a fresh, green patch of land to have his conversation with the Father. He seemed unwilling to be left alone.

I could have sworn there was a hint of terror in his wise, brown eyes. But as quickly as it came, it was replaced with a look of serenity, awareness, and responsibility. I tried my hardest to stay awake, resting against a huge pillar, but he was gone for what seemed like an eternity. I can hardly recall when I shut my eyes, but I remember thinking that it would only be for a moment.

Sleep deprived, I and the other Disciples indulged in a light nap.

When my Master came back from his meditation and prayer he was in an outrage because we had not kept watch over him as we had promised. Sworn to protect my Master under any circumstances, the Messiah took his frustration out on Peter. I had never before seen this side of him or heard him raise his voice in such a way. I think the pressure was starting to get to the Messiah, and that part of him which was human was scared of the mortal death. My Master was afraid of the loneliness and pain that came along with his sacrifice.

I was scared for him.

My Master has told us numerous times:

"Beware the temptations of the flesh because that is what we must fight."

That was undoubtedly the traitor, Judas' downfall. He will never be clean since he let the flesh of a woman come between his love and devotion for my Master! He worshipped Mary Magdalene like a golden goddess, and it devoured him. It was sickening to think about this, and I reveled on my Master's wisdom and knowledge. We must all heed his teachings, unfalteringly.

My Master looked weary, and I realized that he was finding it hard to free himself of his own temptation. Messiah or not, there is an innate selfishness in all of us humans, a desire to live a full, if almost "never-ending" life. This desire consumes us.

Was that what my Master could have been praying about back there in the grassy clearing?

Did he raise his head to the heavens while the other Disciples and I slept, and request salvation from the Father, even though he knew that his time had come? Was he that far gone for an hour or two? Maybe that's why his nerves were so frazzled that night. Could the pressure of the Centurion guards and rabbis hunting us night and day provoke a serious breakdown in his thought process?

Perhaps it did.

It's possible that he could have asked the Father to spare his life and let the cup of sacrifice pass over him, unharmed. His load is much too hard and heavy to carry, nearly impossible for one simple man.

Maybe he was simply savoring his final conversation with the Father before the prophecy began to take its fated course. However, on this night, even the faith he always spoke of may have been wavering in the company of his nearing sacrifice.

My Master must have been going through sheer terror and agony. I don't know what was worse, anticipating the capture and slaughter or the bloodshed itself!

It may sound cruel, but part of me wished that it was all over, so that my Master would not be anticipating the forthcoming horrors.

But all at the same time, I wanted to capture these moments, strenuous as they might be. I wanted to wrap my arms around the Messiah and let him absorb the love and devotion that we all felt for him. That's why we were all here to begin with. He is the reason I abandoned my past life, loved ones, and prospective future. I wanted to believe in love, to believe in the Father and his Son, my Master.

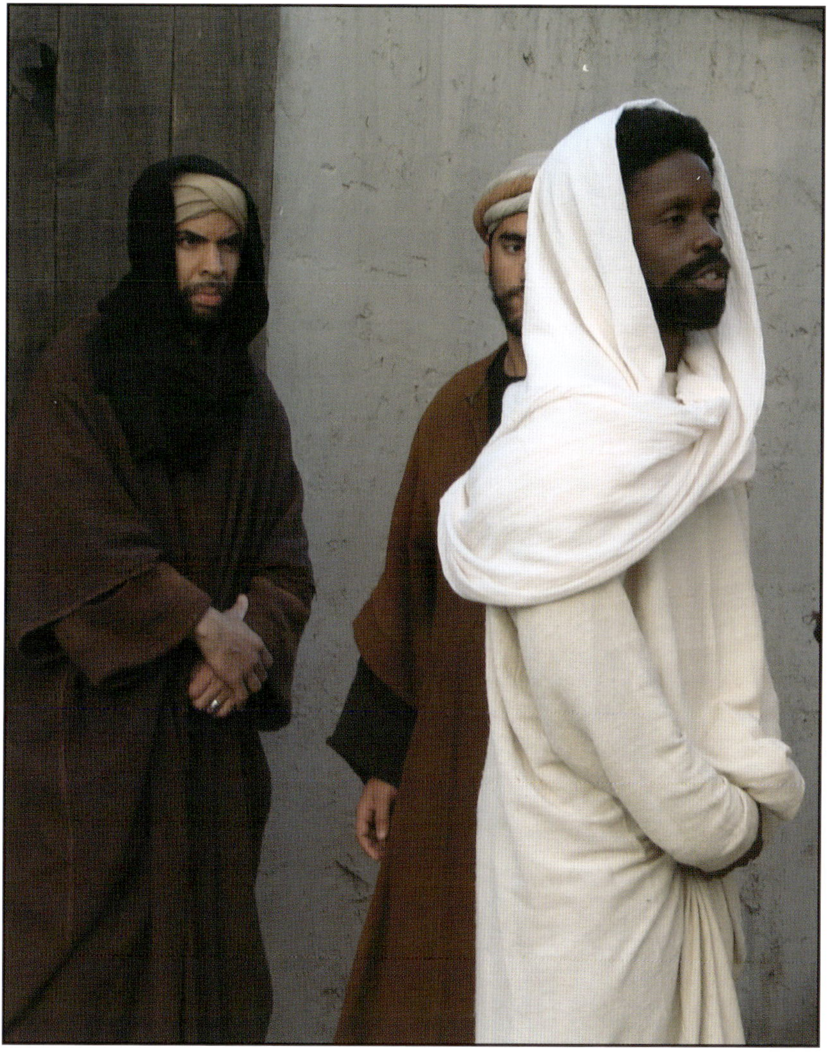

BEFORE I COULD SEE Chapter 16

It seemed only moments ago that I was entirely absorbed with the normalcy of being a simple-minded fisherman. This was before I had been chosen by Joshua, before I could see my true purpose in life. I was tending to the boats, tearing down the mast from a hard afternoon at sea, completely content and ignorant. I couldn't wait to get home, break bread with my family members, and tell them all about another uneventful day. This was the routine I had become accustomed to and I knew nothing more.

I needed nothing more.

But in the very next instant, I was on this amazing, wondrous journey with a man I had never met before, but loved and believed dearly enough to leave everything behind! I remember packing as quickly as I could a single sack of belongings, a cloth-rolled loaf of bread and a large slice of soft, yellow cheese.

My Master told me to leave all the rest of my things behind, as I would not need them where we were going. I kissed my weeping mother and dear sister Rohkl good-bye with tears in my eyes, ready and eager for all that lay ahead of me.

My family understood my cause once they had welcomed and prayed with my Master, and we rejoiced over the last meal that I would share with them. Rohkl was the worst off of us all, since I was her favorite brother and we spent a lot of time together. I protected her from the bullying boys in the neighborhood and taught her how to catch her first salmon.

Everyone could plainly see that my Master was a man destined for greatness, a rabbi blessed to have a gift for deciphering scriptures, with a powerful message to share with all.

They gave me their blessing to go with this man, and help teach his words.

One night in our tent, John shared with me a beautiful passage he had written, starting to tell his own version of our Holy voyage. He said, "For God loved the world so much that he gave his only Son in our place, and who ever believes in him will have eternal, everlasting life."

It was so simple, so pure, and so eloquently put. He knew how to capture the moment and transfer it into eternity.

That verse was immortal.

The gift of poetry was one of the blessings the Father had bestowed upon John, and I will carry that passage in my heart as consolation for the hard and troubled times. For times when my outlook is somber and my prayers are urgent and plentiful.

Times like the present.

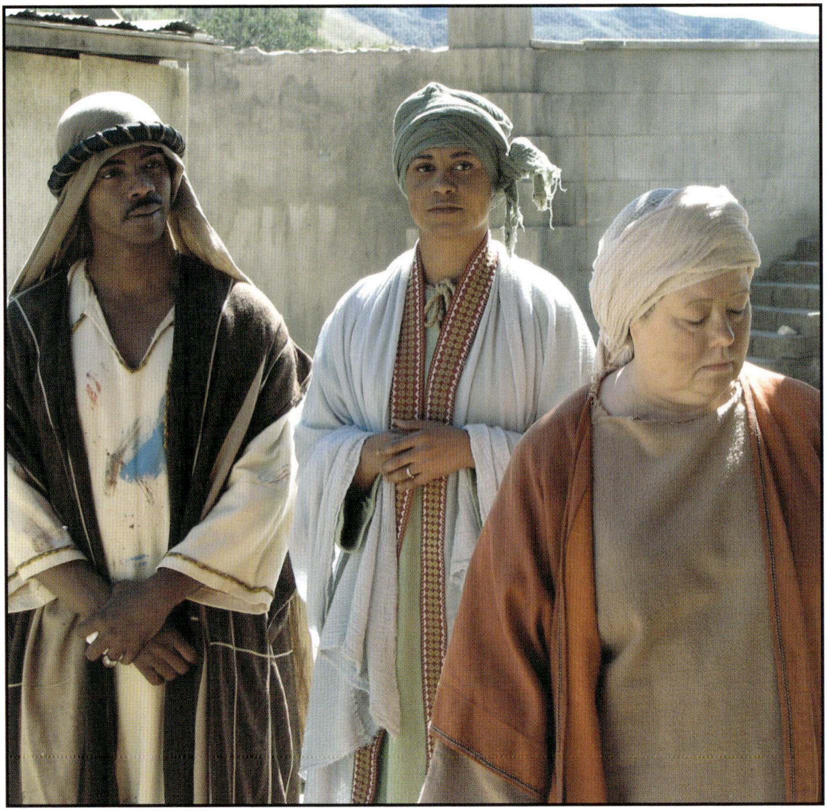

SPREAD THE WORD Chapter 17

My Master now imposes upon us his final request, here in the outskirts of the town. He says, "When I pass from this world, my work and messages must live on. The only way the nonbelievers and doubters will win is if they succeed in silencing my teachings."

He instructs us to tell everyone to sell all of their worldly belongings and use the money they receive from it to spread the message, the word. He tells us to speak in his voice and let our proclamations span from the smallest villages, past the Black Sea, the Mediterranean, and even further!

I am alarmed by the emphasis he places upon this task. I can see one or two of the others becoming nervous upon hearing this as well. We all want to please and fulfill his orders. We know that we must put forth our best efforts to make his last request a reality.

But there are only twelve, no, eleven of us Disciples put together!

This is a very large assignment to undertake. How can we, being of such small numbers, reach and convert a following so massive? It seems nearly impossible. I must remember my faith during times like this.

Who am I, a mere servant, to question his judgments? With newfound resolution, I picture his wishes becoming reality. From our small number, the believers will double, triple and multiply to great heights! The power of his teachings will set many people free.

For generations to come, people will love my Master and speak his truths. They will accept his sacrifice as the blessing it is meant to be, a cleansing of our human sins. The people will observe the day of his passing respectfully, in remembrance.

Soon, huge gatherings will be held all around the world, praising the work of my Master and his Father! It will sweep the nations alarmingly, like a potent, feverish epidemic for which knowledge and prayer is the only cure.

It will be truly magnificent.

We will love one another and be kind to our neighbors, uplifting those plagued with sin and guilt. We will continue to give sight to the blind, hope to the poor and destitute, and good health to the weak and sickly. Our movement will be so powerful that none can deny his teaching!

Large temples will be built in his name, overshadowing any sanctuary constructed before his time. Paintings resembling his mortal image and banners displaying his deeds and words will hang from the walls and doorposts.

All will come to worship and praise his name through song and verse. All will feel welcome and be at peace. Leaders will shed light on ways to surrender to faith, and how to think and act in my Master's likeness.

At these shrines, we believers will find family, fellowship and guidance from teachers and peers alike. None will be denied at the doors to my Master's temple; be them light or dark skinned, old or young, scholarly by profession or carpenter, rich or poor.

I say this because my Master prejudges no one. He loves each and every one of us Disciples equally, patiently, and without blame. I vow to follow in his footsteps and treat every man, woman, and child with the same love and respect my Master had for all humankind. His prayer is that we all may become one: one in the Father, in the Son, and the Holy Spirit.

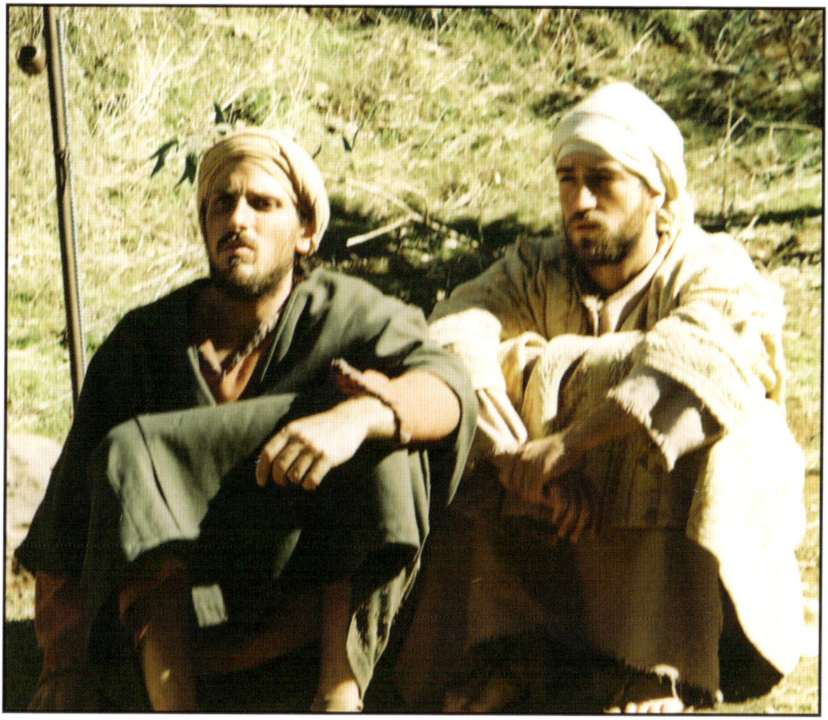

JOURNEYING ON Chapter 18

Refreshed with the knowledge that we are able to keep his words alive, all of us Disciples carry on down the dirt path with a new resolve. We muster up the courage to journey on, we are faithful and willing to aid in the prophecy in whatever way we can. For years I had stood by my Master's side. I had listened to his words, and his voice had become as familiar as my own fathers. Thinking about my Master's fate as we walked along the back roads that night, I reminisced on memories I hadn't thought about since younger days.

I had mourned the death of my grandfather many years ago. I looked up to him dearly, and it was he who impressed upon me the love of the ocean. He taught me all that I knew about being a fisherman. He showed me how to take pride in a living that had sustained my bloodline and the villagers around us for generations.

He was indeed a God-fearing man.

When he passed away, I felt lost for some time. I would often think of him while I worked; casting my nets into the sea, sun in and sun out, smiling up at the sky. I knew that he would be pleased at the way I continued the tradition so willingly.

But it was only after he died that I truly became a man.

I wondered if it would be the same with the passing of my Master, if that would help mold me into a humbler Disciple. I did not want to see my Master suffer, I longed for the Messiah to stay with me here on earth.

I am sure that my brothers felt the same way.

We trudge further into the night, faithfully moving forward along the bramble brush and dirt paths. I hope that we are leading ourselves to freedom, towards some indication of hope and peace. My Master is the Son of the Father, so might there be a chance that the Father will change his mind?

Perhaps there is another way to save the people, an easier and not so ill-fated conclusion. I pray for my Master's body, that it might be spared, that he will live and continue teaching the masses. But I fear such an outcome can never be.

My Master motions for us to rest from our traveling once more and comes around to touch each of our hands. He looks solemnly into our eyes as if attempting to burn our images into his memory as keepsakes for the afterlife. When he stops in front of me, he cups my cheek and says,

"Thomas, I love you. Always remember your faith and everything I have taught you."

"Yes, Master." I reply breathily.

I turn quickly from his gaze, unwilling to break down the way John had done in the presence of the Messiah. After all, my Master's troubles are far greater than my own. It is selfish of me to show weakness when he himself is teetering on edge, as anxious as we all are about what is to come.

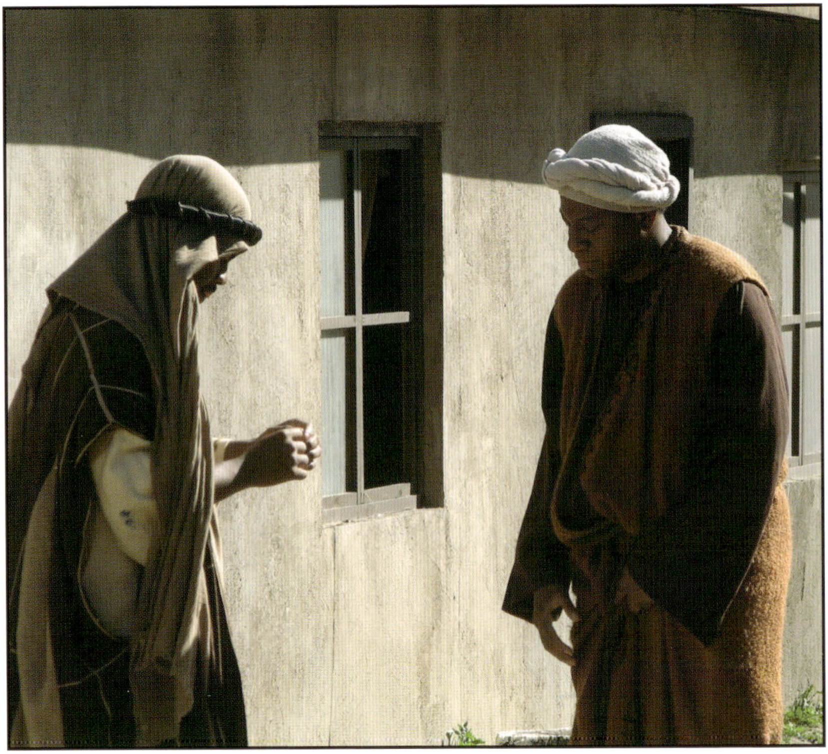

THE TWO HOUSES Chapter 19

My mood is as ever-changing as a gust of the desert winds, and I am glad when my Master starts to retell one of my favorite stories. It is one he often preaches to the masses. I never grow tired of hearing the tale no matter how many times my Master has repeated it.

It went like this: There were two men that wanted to build two houses in their lifetime. They were both beautiful, grand houses, with plenty of room for the men and their families to make into comfortable quarters and sustain them for many years.

One man, thinking not only for the present but for the future, had decided that the best location for his house would be on a plot of solid rock. The only drawback was that there were very few plants and trees that grew out of the rocks. It was a plain, safe place for his family and he was very pleased. He did not feel the need to show the world what a beautiful home he had or impress his guests with his luxury and wealth.

But the other man was of a different opinion.

He wanted to build his house on the ocean shore. That way he would be entitled to the very best view, and could in turn be seen by people in all directions. He wanted everyone to know what an extravagant kingdom he had built for himself and the rest of his family. He was also very pleased.

The two men were acquaintances who spoke often in passing, and struck up a conversation one day in regards to their new properties. The man who was building his house near the ocean guffawed with laughter at the other man's choice. He told the other man that he had made a terrible mistake. No trees? No grass? How would any of the townspeople see what the man had created if he was living in such humble surroundings?

But the man who was building his house on the rocks just smiled, tilting his head to one side silently. When he spoke it was in a low, friendly tone. He told the man who was going to build his house on the sea that the reason he decided to build his house on the rocks was because stability and practicality came before showmanship in his eyes, and in the Father's eyes. The man who was going to build his house on the sand didn't think much of the others reasoning.

The two men shook hands and parted ways.

Before long, just as they had planned, both men had constructed their homes and moved their families into their havens. The man who built his house on the rocks took his time, laying the stones brick by brick, putting each one in their perfect niche. He built a medium-sized home, round and cozy, with just enough room for man, woman and child.

However, the man who was building his house on the sand used another approach. He aspired to have the tallest, most wonderful house in the area! He wanted people to gaze at his palace from miles away. He rushed to build the first floor, laying the stones unevenly, cementing the base of the house sloppily.

He built his fortress 5 stories high, with a glorious tower at the top to finish the elaborate building. The paint was bright and colorful, very modern and unconventional. Inside hung many Jewish tapestries and homely comforts, in excess of what was needed for the man and his wife.

People came from far and wide to comment on the man's beach front home, and he was very proud. All seemed well, and the men crossed each other's paths once more, relaying all that they had discovered during their efforts.

Once again, the men shook hands and parted ways.

But then something unexpected happened. A great storm was brewing and the people of the town were forced to take cover! Even the elderly could not recall a time when the rain was so relentless. Whipping winds could be seen forming by the far depths of the ocean and were quickly making their way towards the village.

The two men hurriedly took shelter in their newly constructed homes. The man who built his house on the rocks was grateful for his choice and knew that his family would be very safe there. He prayed to the Father to watch over him during the storm, confident that Jehovah would watch over him at all times.

But the man who built his house on the sand was worried. The winds had picked up speed and were coming towards his house at a furious pace. He locked all of the doors and secured the windows, but the rain was relentless.

He was regretful for mocking the man who built his house on the rocks, and realized he should have been more humble and practical about the matter. Due to his pride, the man and his wife's safety were now at stake!

The hour grew late and all became dark.

In the morning the sun rose on a beautiful village. Every sign of the storm was gone and the townspeople breathed a sign of relief. The men and women came out of their homes and the children ran and played on the streets. The man who built his house on the rocks came outside with his wife and child, smiling up at the sky, and blessing the Father for keeping them safe throughout the turbulent night.

Everything seemed well and the day went on as usual.

Suddenly, a young boy came running through the streets, alerting all villagers in his path of the horrible news.

"The colorful house on the ocean has fallen! He said. Everything has crumbled. The high tower is nothing but broken debris on the beach! The man and his wife are nowhere to be seen!"

All of the villagers, including the man that had built his house upon the rocks, came to see what was left of the man's home. Just as the boy had described, there was hardly anything left to be seen: the tapestries had been defaced by the cruel storm, and a few colored stones, bits of furniture, and broken stained glass pieces had formed an ugly pile of debris on the beach.

That afternoon, the villagers held a ceremony in remembrance of the man and his wife.

The parallels in this detailed story are related to faith and humility. All who love the Messiah and make their decisions based upon his love will be saved when the storm comes to wreck and ravage our souls. It is our duty to nurture our faith and hope in the Father and the Messiah.

Often, our pride can lead us to believe that our faith is stronger and more durable than it actually is. Only when we are faced with adversity do we realize just how shaky it may be. I can only hope that my foundation stands strong when they finally come for my Master.

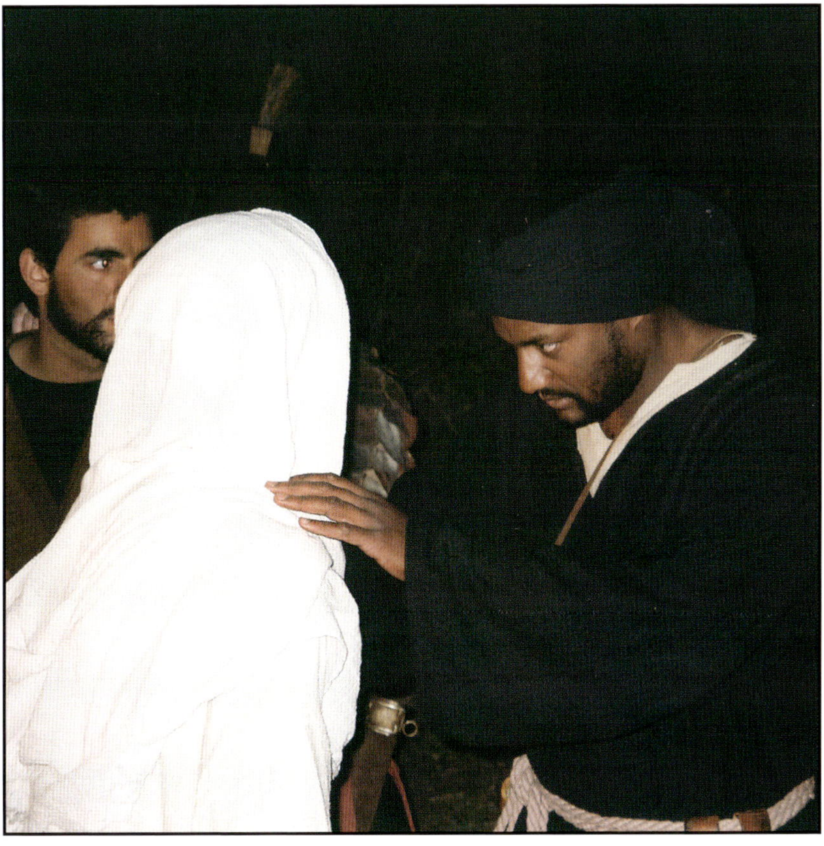

CORNERED Chapter 20

It happens far more quickly than I ever imagined. My Master begins to lead us in a rousing hymnal while we rest and we all lift our voices in praise of the Father's works. Then suddenly, a rustling in the bushes below gives way to shouts from bellowing voices.

The Romans have caught up with us!

Peter and John, closest to the commotion, quickly draw their swords and run to stand in front of my Master. It seems that John has discovered his bravery after all, indeed when it is needed the most. Simon and I quickly motion for the others to create a barrier between the approaching Centurion guards and my Master.

My heart races wildly as I'm sure do the other Disciples. What we had thought were a handful of armed guards was turning out to be a huge number, with the infamous Horatius leading the way! This does not look well for my Master.

What to do in this situation? We had known all along that we were to be faced with this danger, but little can prepare us for the terror of the Romans brandishing their sharp, steel edged swords and yelling orders out to the other guards. We are cornered, helpless.

"Drop all weapons!" one says.

I am not even carrying a small hunting knife on my person, so used to prayer and peace have I become. However, some of my other brothers nervously drop their own. Bartholomew, wielding a huge wooden plank, is the only one besides Peter and John who pretend not to hear the order.

"Secure the area!" another guard shouts.

"Oh dear Father, please protect us! Shield your Son in the face of danger," I pray silently.

I look to my Master, hidden near the back of the group, his lips moving softly in prayer as well. The expression on his face is serene. I can tell that finally, the Messiah is willing and accepting of being delivered.

A great sorrow overcomes me, and I hold back an urge that begs me to reach out and touch him. Any indication or expression of joy or pain will certainly tip off the Roman guards to his identity. It is only a matter of time before they discover him on their own. Perhaps we can stall the process by diverting their attention or confusing them!

Then suddenly, an all too familiar face is pushed forward through the crowd and my bright idea is doused, an unexpected downpour sprinkled onto a porch-lit lamp. Judas! The traitor has not only alerted the rabbis and officials to our whereabouts, but he himself leads the Centurion guards to our Master!

I am disgusted by the shameless rat. My Master sees Judas in the crowd of Romans, and a look of great sadness passes over his face. Judas is an unfaithful son, plotting against his father for the family inheritance. I wonder what that must feel like on Judas' end. What must it be like to know that you are murdering the Son of the Father, the Messiah, and you are fated to burn in the afterlife for all of eternity? He does not look well at all, and I wonder if perhaps he is pondering the very same thing.

Then, one of the Roman guards, I believe his name is Malchus, barks expectantly at all of us. He demands to know which one of us is Joshua of Nazareth, the dark-skinned Jew who claims to the Son of God. He tells us that whoever the false prophet is should step forward at this time, in the name of the King, Caesar.

Lost for words and direction, all of us Disciples timidly stop in our tracks. No one makes a sound and the Romans become angered.

"I know you can hear me Jews!" Malchus bellows. Now which one of you is he?"

My Master steps forward, and my heart feels as if it is pounding loud enough for the world to hear. Momentarily I feel my senses failing me and I become lightheaded, but I fight the urge to collapse with weakness.

"I am he," says my Master.

Peter, defender of my Master's safety, attempts to come to the Messiah's aid, perhaps for the last time. Still holding his sword in the air, he bravely stands in front of my Master, his head raised defiantly. I wonder what he is thinking, for the Roman soldiers greatly outnumber the rest of us and Horatius is no fool with a weapon!

Then Peter speaks. He says, "He lies! I am Joshua."

For one small moment, I have hope. Perhaps his tactics will work! Although he will be sacrificing himself, he will allow my Master his freedom. Surely Peter would be rewarded in heaven for such bravery? Perhaps this is a way for the word to be altered, with a selfless sacrifice from one of my Master's Disciples! But the feeling is short-lived. Horatius points his great, bejeweled sword straight at Peter's heart, not believing his claims for a moment.

"How can you be the Messiah? You are not Black, Jew!" he sneers.

Peter hangs his head, defeated. Having heard enough, Horatius demands the soldiers to move in and arrest all of us Disciples. Once we are incarcerated, they will discover who the Black "Messiah" truly is.

No doubt we will all be tortured and killed.

Suddenly my Master steps forward and addresses the Roman guards.

"I am he. Let the others go that the word will be fulfilled" he says.

Upon hearing this, the Roman Guards start mumbling amongst themselves, asking Horatius what they should do. They stare at the Messiah blankly. Then, Horatius grabs Judas by the collar of his tunic and flings him onto the ground before us. He sarcastically orders the betrayer to do what he has come to do and rightfully earn his thirty pieces of silver.

We each look upon this man, our sworn and dedicated "brother" with pure disgust and disillusion. He would betray our beloved Messiah for a meager thirty pieces of silver? Peter lets out an exclamation of anguish, and, if not for the Romans surrounding us, would murder the hideous snake I am sure of it!

Judas slowly rises from the ground, his hands covered with dust, lips chapped and eyes sunken. I could have sworn his body was trembling and it seems as if he has not anticipated the difficulty of following through with his greedy plans. I feel no empathy for him.

Step by step, each foot heavier than the next, he makes his way towards my Master. You can hear a coin drop in the desert, the silence in the air is so clear and terrible. I feel rooted to the ground, completely immobile, as if watching the whole experience from an outside point of view.

I now think desperately to myself, "Please Judas, I pray of you, do not do this! My Master has done nothing but speak the truth. I cannot bear to be without him. We cannot continue to teach his words in the same way, we are not the Messiah! "

But my prayers go unanswered. For there is no huge bolt of lighting that has come to strike the traitor down, incapacitating him, and no stray arrow shot from a wandering marauder that renders him motionless. Yes, Judas of Iscariot is intent on revealing my Master's identity to the Centurion guards.

Slowly, methodically, Judas raises his head as he came closer to my Master. As he brushes my shoulder in passing, I see that he has broken into a cold sweat. He stops in front of my Master and pauses, breathing heavily.

Horatius begins to lose patience with Judas' dramatic, drawn out antics and threatens him with force from a distance. He yells out to Judas, wondering aloud if the ex-follow may be having second thoughts, as traitors often do. He sarcastically invites Judas to join the rest of us Disciples in following the false "Messiah" to his grave. If he so chooses, the betrayer will be given the same treatment as any other dirty "Black Jew lover". Judas is only useful to the Romans if he aids in capturing my Master, nothing more.

"And even that may change, depending on your actions, Jew!" Horatius snorts. Mark my words."

Horatius tells Judas that he will pay greatly for his disobedience if he does not comply immediately with their agreement. Judas will feel the pain of the lash man's whip and then be sentenced to the same fate as the Messiah himself! He will be left for twenty days and nights inside of a black hole before sentencing, a punishment commonly used to torture prisoners with its stifling surroundings, driving them mad. As if this is not enough to convince Judas to follow through with has been planned, Horatius adds nastily that the thirty pieces of silver will dangle from a string on Judas' neck!

Judas' body visibly stiffens with tension at the threats, and he turns to look at my Master intently. Then, as gently as a mother stooping to bestow a loving token of affection onto her infant's precious forehead, Judas kisses my Master delicately on his right cheek.

The other Disciples and I know at once that Judas' feinted act of affection must be the signal the Roman guards are waiting for. My Master tilts his head and an odd expression contorts his kind features.

"You betray me with a kiss?" my Master whispers.

In a motion that, even in betrayal seems unlike the Messiah, he wildly throws Judas' body away from him and into the soldier's arms. Aghast, I watch, afflicted. But as quickly as it has come, a demure but doleful countenance replaces the enraged look on my Master's face.

My soul weeps as I witness my Master's obvious defeat. The Roman soldiers close in on us, but I am in such a state of misery that I cannot become further alarmed. What is meant to occur is ordained by the Father, I think to myself. My Master and mentor has been discovered and captured by one of his own, tossed to the Romans and the Sanhedrin! He is at their mercy now.

The Centurion guards continue advancing towards Peter and John. I see no glint of fear in either man's eye, and then Peter raises his sword high in the air, shouting out his love for my Master. Malchus, his sights set on teaching Peter a lesson, growls ominously and is headed straight for him!

Reacting swiftly, Peter swings his weapon in one quick motion and sliced Malchus' earlobe, detaching it from his body! Paralyzed, Malchus drops to the ground, clutching the bloody, mangled stub of an ear. The sounds that come out of the man's mouth are agonizing.

My Master quickly walks over to where Peter stands and picks up the disconnected earlobe. He kneels next to Malchus and prays to the Father. He places his hands next to the gushing wound, and re-attaches the Centurion's ear! Even in the midst of those seeking to persecute my Master, he allows himself to heal and forgive, continuing to prove that he is the true Messiah.

The next thing that happens is truly miraculous. It is apparent that Malchus is unable to contain himself, forgetting his place and the people around him. He bows his head onto the ground and kissed the Messiah's feet.

He cries out uncontrollably and the tears stream down his face. Disciples and Centurions alike are astonished.

"Messiah!" he says.

He professes his love for my Master and tells him that he and his family will be faithful followers in this life and in the next! My Master blesses Malchus and then rises from the ground. The other Romans are confused, not wanting to believe their own eyes.

Did they just witness one of the famed healings that has caused so much controversy? Why would one of their own guards become a believer of the Black Messiah? They are dumfounded. Could he possibly be speaking and teaching the truth? This is far too much for them to comprehend and they mumble to one another, swords cocked offensively in the evening sky.

My Master raises his hands in the air and speaks firmly.

"Enough!" My Master says. I'll go peacefully. I will not resist."

I think to myself, here it is, this is the end. All that we have been working towards, everything that we have accomplished as a unit is now past.

Then, a shout from the mountainside can be heard.

It sounds like women's voices echoing in the distance! Who can that be? It is unsafe and unheard of for women to be traveling on the back roads of any town and I can scarcely imagine any lady would know her way through the hills of Gethsemane, especially in the dark.

The shadowy figures soon become clearer and I realize that it is my Master's mother Mary, and Mary Magdalene who have sought us out! No doubt the women have come to warn the Messiah of the Roman guard's proximity, but alas, they have not reached us in time. Mary Magdalene must have been leading the way, since her profession demands knowledge of many routes in surrounding villages.

When they come close enough to see what has developed, they are stricken with suffering. Mary, my Master's mother, is paralyzed with emotion and cries out to her firstborn child.

"Joshua!"

Some of the soldiers surround them, blocking their way. Mary Magdalene attempts to part through the guards, but they detain her forcefully. Horatius remarks nastily to Mary Magdalene that he is not opposed to using violence on a Nazareen loving wench! She becomes silent, her eyes throwing daggers at the detestable Roman guard.

She then whispers dejectedly:

"It is too late".

A number of Centurion guards isolate my Master as we watch, painfully aware that we are unable to help the Messiah any longer. Some of the men closing in on him chuckle eagerly, delighted to be a part of such an important Roman victory. This will bring them much glory and they will be looked upon favorably for many years to come.

They bind my Master's loving hands and feet, handling him harshly in the process. They tighten the knots so strongly, more than is necessary, and the ropes draw blood, the first abrasions inflicted on my Master's body.

I fear they not be the last.

When they finally carry him away I feel as if I have been robbed of something, so attached am I to my Master. The others and I sink to the ground helplessly. We sit there for many hours, distraught.

There is nothing more to be done, we have lost our earthly King.

94 Color Of The Cross

ALL HAIL CAESAR Chapter 21

By the time the sun came up this morning, the capture of my Master, Joshua of Nazareth, was on every villager's lips. Now mid-afternoon, all of us Disciples have heard that the Messiah is to be tried in Gethsemane. We have split up into smaller groups as we approach the crowds, attempting to draw very little attention. The people are angry at my Master for reasons I cannot fathom, thirsty for his blood to be shed.

For the sentencing of My Master's crucifixion, the Messiah is brought before the Governor of the Roman Province of Judea, Pontius Pilate. Curiously, Pilate has not chosen to side with the Roman guards, or the Sanhedrin's view of my Master's position. He feels that my Master has done nothing to deserve death and attempts to reason with the leading priests.

He asks them why they wish for this man's death. They reply that he should die because he wrongly claims to be King of the Jews, for a Black Nazareen is far from holy. Their transparent detest for my Master is insidiously blatant, even to Pontius Pilate.

It has been rumored that earlier, Pilate took my Master, Joshua of Nazareth, aside and spoke with him. He pleaded with the man to share with him any information or defense that could save my Master. He asked my Master if he knew who Pontius Pilate was and what he represented. For Pilate had the power to either save my Master's life or sentence him to a vengeful ending.

My Master then replied that Pilate had no power over him whatsoever. Any commands he was allotted to sentence my Master were given from above, from the Father himself. There was nothing that a mere man could do to condemn or save the Messiah. No, the King of the Jews was destined only for what the Father had ordained.

The weight of my Master's words and the nonsensical orders from Caiaphas and the Sanhedrin make Pontius Pilate nervous. Pilate attempts to dig deeper into my Master's story in order to better understand the "how's" and "why's" this man has come to be judged. Ultimately, my Master asks nothing of the Governor. He does not proclaim his innocence or beg for his life to be spared.

The Roman official has never witnessed anything of the sort in all of his years. He is at a crossroads within himself, not wanting to persecute the innocent. However, both the Sanhedrin and the villagers hate this man. They all but beg for his death, by the hundreds and thousands.

It is alarming to the Governor.

For my Master's unassuming presence and kind voice most certainly touched Pilate if the gossip proves to be true, and he must be made uneasy by the Sanhedrin's findings. Some people say that he has set his mind on releasing my Master peacefully, for he does not want the Messiah's blood on his own hands. I pray that he fights valiantly for my Master's freedom.

It is said that he pondered my Master's words and all of the possibilities to himself in a dark room.

"My Kingdom is not of this world," my Master had said to him. "If my Kingdom were of this world my servants would fight, so that I should not be delivered to the Jews; but now my Kingdom is not from here." Pilate was stunned by his answers.

Indeed there was something different about this man. What if this Joshua of Nazareth spoke the truth? What if the King of the Jews had rightfully come into this world in the body of a dark skinned Savior? So far as Pilate could tell the man had committed no plausible crimes and was a peaceful person. He decided then that he would do all he could to protect the strange prophet. If the people would not let the man go unharmed, then Pilate would rule as mildly as he was allowed.

Upon hearing the outcome the Governor has chosen, the Sanhedrin become outraged. They use the Roman King, Caesar Augustus, as a scapegoat for wanting my Master's death. Pontius Pilate, not knowing what other avenue to pursue, decides to present my Master in front of the unruly crowds.

He introduces my Master to the thousands that have come to see and participate in the Messiah's sentencing. But the fickle villagers will no longer accept the Messiah. Many who had praised him for his works now callously dismiss him!

They senselessly chant out ill wishes for my Master as if fueled by an evil and convincing spirit. Do they not remember all the good my Master has done for them? Only one week ago they had welcomed us into their arms, proclaiming love for his word and deeds. They sought counseling and healing from his blessed hands. Their allegiance had been akin to idolatry, and the guidance that the Messiah gave to them was received as automatically as one takes in a breath of air.

How quickly the people have forgotten all that my Master has given them! He asks nothing in return from them, save allegiance and faith in his principles. However, Satan has taken hold of their thoughts; they are unable to deliver on their promises.

My Master, along with us Disciples, has exhausted his body over the years. We have spent hours conducting healings for these ungrateful people! The miracles we have been blessed to perform forces us to expend all of our energy, and many of us have collapsed for hours after the crowds disperse.

I can scarcely believe my own ears! At times when I feel like my feet are so blistered and swollen that I cannot not go on, a single thought about the lives we help save and the people that have been moved by the Messiah's words keep me walking.

Looking around at the driven and angry mob that thirsts for my Master's elimination, I realize there is no longer any hope. The only purpose I have left to fulfill, having been stripped of my dignitary, is to inform those with open ears of all that my Master wishes to impress upon the world. I stand off to the side of the crowd with my head wrapped in heavy material, incognito.

"We have no King but Caesar, all hail Caesar!" the Sanhedrin shouts.

"Kill the rebel claiming to be the black King of the Jews!" the villagers echo.

One woman that is heard crying hysterically catches my attention, jolting me out of my own thoughts. She has fallen onto the ground in a physical tantrum, unable to control her spasms. One or two villagers are attempting to silence her obnoxious cries, but are unsuccessful in their efforts. I peer at her intently and noticed a recognizable cinnamon strand of hair peeking from beneath the folds of cloth around her neckline.

Mary of Magdalene!

The other two women must be Joshua's dear mother, Mary, and one of my Master's other kin. Beside themselves with sorrow, their lamenting still does not rival Mary Magdalene's anguish. Her relationship with my Master has altered the way she views the world. He has forged an outlet for this woman's soul, allowing her to love and grow with the strength of his words.

Although I would never speak of this while the others and I were following my Master across the lands, I do believe that Mary Magdalene may be my Master's most loyal believer. She is the only person that can compare spoken translations of the sacred teachings to my Master's own.

The sounds of her sobbing personify my desolation.

Pilate, fearing the people will not back down from their raving, offers up another solution. He does not wish to inflict pain upon my Master, but the people speak clearly, and it is violence that they want. Pontius Pilate, at his wits end, beseeches the people to settle for a lesser evil. Why not resolve the issue by beating this Joshua of Nazareth for his supposed insolence?

Surely this will be enough to quell their disputes with the poor man!

Without a second thought, the people begin screaming and throwing small stones or rubbish onto the platform where my Master is being tried. They do not seem satisfied with a simple beating. Does Pontius Pilate not realize the severity of the situation? Is he blind to the wrong-doings that Joshua of Nazareth has performed?

In the opinion of the crowds, my Master has committed high treason by blaspheming the teachings of the Torah by his color, popularity, and presence. All that he represents is an insult to the people and the Sanhedrin. They vehemently demand the highest punishment possible of the Roman official.
They will stop at nothing to insure my Master's death!

In his defense, Pilate fights for my Master's, marveling at the man's integrity and wisdom. He tries to reason with the crowds and strike up some sort of compromise. Their deafening screams become more and more uncontrollable.

There, in plain view of thousands, having been abandoned by his beloved Disciples and the people that have so fiercely worshipped him, my Master is sentenced to the beginning stages of agony. Even though I was fully aware that my Master is destined for this, I cannot believe what I am hearing.

Pilate's mouth seems to be moving in slow motion and it is hard for my brain to comprehend all that he is ordering.

Pilate announces to the crowd that Joshua of Nazareth, the man claiming to be the dark-skinned King of the Jews, will be subjected to flogging, as penalty for blaspheming the scriptures of the Torah.

Pilate also firmly states that he sees little fault with my Master. He indemnifies himself against any proclamations that the governor has killed the so-called "King of the Jews". It is the people, the rabbis and the villagers that seek my Master's blood, and only through their wishes is he sentenced in such a way.

Pontius Pilate thinks the Sanhedrin's desire to end my Master's life is a travesty. He sees the jealousy that they display, but can do nothing to save my Master from their blood-thirsty ways. There is another man on trial that day, and he is called the name Barabbus. Barabbus is a man who has committed uncountable sins against the Torah, and is a well know thief, liar and murderer.

Pontius Pilate agrees to release either my Master or Barabbus on that day. Pilate hopes that the Sanhedrin and the villagers will have mercy upon this man, Joshua of Nazareth, and choose to set him free. After all, my Master is no violent murderer, and surely the people will not want Barabbas amongst them?

Pilate has two Roman guards bring Barabbas onto the platform where he stands, addressing the crowd. He announces Barabbas' lengthy list of crimes to all. Some know the reputation that precedes the cold criminal and yells of distaste are heard from the crowd.

Barabbas is a large, scraggly-haired man with a face hidden underneath a braided beard and thick eyebrows. His biceps and frame are enough to make even the strong wary, and his gaze is steady, fearing no one. He nonchalantly stares at the Sanhedrin and the villagers, only changing his expression to growl at the yelling crowd.

I pray more fiercely than ever before that the people will release my Master. It is obvious that this Barabbas is a threat to all of Judea! If he is let loose, he will likely kill or rape that very night! Why would the Sanhedrin want this man on the streets, he is insane!

The crowds begin whispering amongst themselves, buzzing excitedly. I can tell that Barabbas makes them uncomfortable and they know that their home may be the next one struck by his hand. The Sanhedrin, however, does not blink or twitch an eyelid. They have their sights set on my Master's annihilation.

This is obvious.

Caiaphus, the leader and High Priest of the Sanhedrin, asks Pilate for a moment to speak to the people. This is not the usual way of sentencing a man, and Pilate declines his suggestion. This angers Caiaphus in such a way that he pulls Pilate aside and speaks to him heatedly. He tells Pilate that the Sanhedrin, the people, and God have ordained for this man to be killed for his bold blasphemy.

He also reminds Pilate that the crowds had sworn that only Caesar is their King, and it should not matter what will be done with Judea's own! Caiaphus also informs Pilate that it will not go over very well for the governor if he does not comply with the Sanhedrin's wishes. He asks Pilate if he understands and Pilate nods.

Unable to stand up for a man that is not of his own lineage and confronted by a nation and their leading officials, Pontius Pilate announces to the masses that Barabbas is released and Joshua of Nazareth, the Black King of the Jews, is sentenced to death by crucifixion.

John, standing next to me wrapped in similar garb, crumbles visibly, whimpering with shock. I brace myself for the horrible things I am about to witness. Only the Father can help his Son now.

102 Color Of The Cross

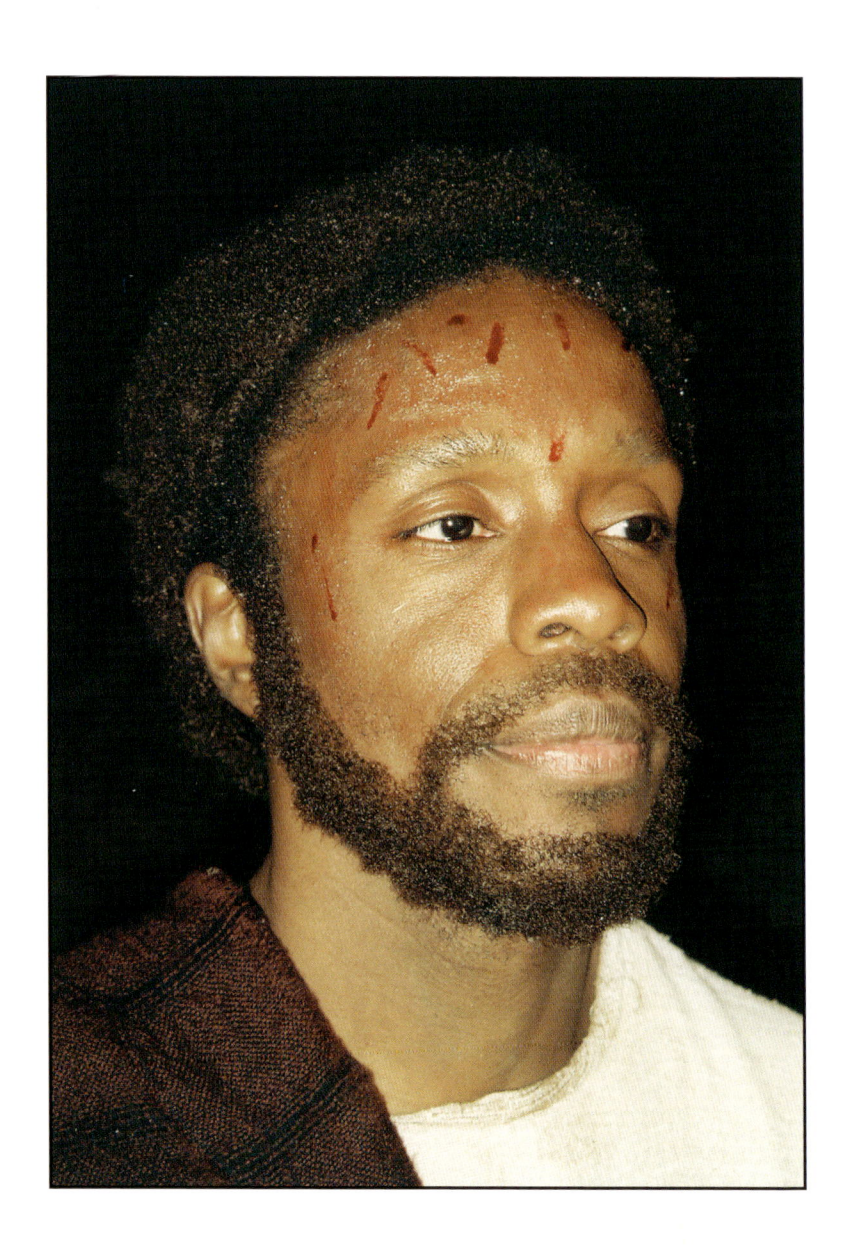

THE AGONY OF JOSHUA Chapter 22

As soon as my Master's feet hit the stone pavement, the villagers jeer obnoxiously, spitting on his body and throwing spoiled fruits in his direction.

The Roman guards handle him roughly, dragging him barefoot along the cobblestone for almost one quarter of a mile. It is hard to keep my Master in full view. There are so many people in the crowd and everyone wants to see his suffering firsthand.

John and I weave in and out of the crowds and it is lucky for us that we are both of lean builds. John is the one who leads the way since his frame is almost childlike, and I hold fast to his robes so that we will not be separated.

I cannot leave my Master alone like this; I have to see the prophecy out until it is finished. I hope that he will somehow be able to feel our presence, and that the Father will make his sacrifice as painless as possible.

Perhaps he will pass quickly by some unforeseen complication.

We run harder, out of breath but determined to stay in the forefront. The Centurion guards have led my Master to an all too familiar clearing, and John and I look at one another worriedly. Prisoners and criminals are brought to this place to be beaten and flogged.

Many people have been sentenced to this torture as a capital punishment in its own right, but for my Master, this is simply the beginning.

One of the guards is kicking my Master in the shins, urging him to move faster towards a pole with metal fixtures (in which to weave strands of rope for a prisoner's feet and hands.) The only Centurion that is not particularly enthusiastic in leading my Master is Malchus, whom my Master had healed only hours before. I can see masked admiration in his gaze; he is only going through the motions of torture for the sake of his country and fellow comrades. He bows his head and I see his lips moving, he is asking the Father for forgiveness!

Then, a monstrous soldier with large biceps and a black mask comes and stands next to the other Romans, removing a hand-woven, black leather flagellum from a velvet bag. Its tentacles are revealed and the coils of the whip are braided tightly; attached to the knot at each end are sharp pieces of metal and glass, carefully melted and sanded into the shape of a triangle.

I draw in a harsh, shallow breath.

Horatius grabs my Master by each ear and, perhaps thinking it will humor the crowd, bangs my Master's head against the pole before his flogging. He does this three times in a row and by the third time, my Master has blood trickling out of his right ear. A single tear comes down the side of his otherwise expressionless face.

I cannot recall ever seeing my Master cry before.

Horatius then binds my Master's hands and feet with rope and attached the ropes to the pole, with my Master's chest and body facing towards the pole. He takes a knife from under his belt, and I think surely he is going to stab my Master in the stomach, but instead, he swiftly cuts away my Master's robe and undergarments so that the Messiah is naked to the world.

More humiliating to me than this poor fisherman has words to describe, this receives much laughter from the crowds. They cheer Horatius' efforts in the name of Caesar. Even though my Master will endure much more than ridicule, I am embarrassed that they choose to expose my Master in such a way. He has done little to deserve hatred, why must he anger the crowd so?

I am now fully aware of the power of envy and prejudice.

This ordeal in its entirety came about solely because the matrimony of the Sanhedrin and all that they represent, in their minds, must never be questioned. They use my Master's appearance and popularity with the people to turn his followers against the Messiah, and it is nothing short of disgusting! It is easier to target my Master because he is a Black Jew. Truly they are born of the devil himself!

After preparing my Master for the flogging, the huge Roman guard speaks loudly to all who are present. He announces that my Master, Joshua of Nazareth, is sentenced to thirty-nine lashes from the flagellum for claiming to be a false Messiah, and wickedly misleading a portion of the Jewish nation. The people cheer, wanting to see more of my Master's suffering. They wanted to partake fully in the agony of Joshua of Nazareth, my Master.

Thirty-nine lashes? This is more than barbaric, the maximum number of lashes allowed in Judea! I can scarcely imagine what that might feel like. I pray to the heavens above that they may show my Master some mercy, and perhaps lessen the blows in some way.

Now the guard begins to whip the Messiah.

One! Two! Three! Four!

On the fifth whipping, my Master cries out in pain. Anguished, John takes my hand and squeezes it in his own. However, he does not look away from my Master's direction for even a moment.

Six! Seven! Eight! Nine!

Oh Father, have mercy! My Master's exclamations are low-pitched and guttural. By the twenty fifth lashing, I can no longer see the muscles in my Master's back and legs, they are a mess of blood and torn flesh. The gashes are at least two inches deep, and every time the whip comes around once more, it cuts deeper and deeper into the same open wounds!

Twenty-eight! Twenty-nine! Thirty!

My Master, unable to hold his weight up against the frightful whipping, collapses onto his knees, and the ropes cut deeply into his wrists and ankles. After what feels like an eternity, the ogre-like guard withdraws the whips from my Master, finished with this portion of the sentencing.

My Master is released from the bindings and lies on the ground, near motionless. I look to the sky, wishing an angel would strike down upon these Roman brutes, and free my Master of his confines. Then a swarm of hungry, yellow mosquitoes passes over my Master's head. Upon discovering the gold mine that is my Master's backside they attack him, buzzing greedily as they sink their needles into his open wounds, sucking on the free-flowing liquid until their tiny bodies became hopelessly engorged and appear drunk with satiation, much like the crowds witnessing my Master's torture.

Will this day never end?

I kick a rock on the ground, swearing obscenities, frustrated at my helplessness. An old woman sees me doing this and points me out to those around her. She whispers to her husband, and he along with his son approach me.

"Are you a friend of this black-skinned fool?" the husband asks.

"If you are, speak now, so that we may punish you as well! Every last one of his followers deserves to be beaten bloody!" his son adds menacingly.

John has walked a few paces from me, so he is safe from confrontation for the moment. I want to stand up for my Master more than anything. It is my desire to speak truthfully throughout wind, rain, or natural disaster! I long to meet fists with these two men who mock the Messiah's words, but I cannot.

I am afraid.

I tell myself that it is not fear but loyalty to my Master's bidding that we must all survive to spread his message. However, faced with a crowd that seeks death for my leader, I feel anything but steel resolve planted in my gut.

I do not want them to know that I have been part of my Masters movement. If I confess, I will be a target for violence and even death! The crowds are enormous and I am but one man. If they can condemn my Master in such a way, they surely will have no problem delivering my body as well; for I am sure my brothers will not come to my aid!

I do not know what to say. Should I save myself, or proclaim my devotion?

I open my mouth, and tell a bold-faced lie. I tell them that I am against the false prophet and have never laid eyes on him before in my life. Furthermore, stating that the reason I seem upset is because I had placed a bet on the length of the blasphemer's life. I tell them that the Black scavenger has already outlived my marker, and I have lost ten pieces of silver!

I cannot believe the words that are coming out of my mouth and as I speak I can hear our Master's prophecy at what I now know was our last supper with him. My Master had been correct about his Disciples disowning him and his teachings. I will be forever ashamed that I did not hold fast to his words, announcing my love for the Messiah. The older man and his son chuckle and pat me on the back reassuringly. After they walk away, I hang my head in self-loathing.

I look towards the place where my Master has collapsed. The Romans are already poking and prodding at his poor, assaulted body, egging him on with their embittered commentary. They yell for him to stand upright and walk along the stone path. Can they not see that my Master is in no state to keep moving? Those lashes would have imposed upon a lesser man the stroke of death! In crazed desperation, I pray that my Master's heart will fail him before the worst of it is to come.

Alas, my Master is given little time to recover; the Roman guards have him staggering to his feet only moments after the flogging. A teenage boy throws a succession of colored glass marbles that hit my Master on the neck and head, and the boy is rewarded with infectious laughter by all who watch his childish prank.

Yet another group begins chanting out loud and making fun of my Master's appearance.

"Kill the Dirty King!!!"

"Save yourself if you can, Dark Prince!"

"Maybe your father, the Devil, will rise up from the murky depths and redeem your tainted soul. If you are the Son of God, why would he not choose to save you? I can only imagine that he is as black and homely as his offspring!"

The Centurions allow the villagers to pinch my Master as they walk along the roads. The look on my Master's face is one of pain and bewilderment and I long to reach out and reassure him. As this thought crosses my mind, an elderly lady approaches my Master and smiles vibrantly.

The old woman stops directly in front of the Messiah and bows her head in what looks like a prayer. She cradles my Master's face in her hands and he visibly softens. I am touched by this moment and thank the Father for this small blessing. The woman releases her caress a moment later, slapping my Master boldly across each cheek! After doing so, she spits into his hair, cursing him and all that he has taught.

She loudly announces that her once God-fearing first-born son had met and broken bread with my Master one year ago and had begun to reject the old ways for my Master's teachings. She yells that she will sleep peacefully only once he burns in the afterlife!

Is there no mercy for the weak and persecuted?

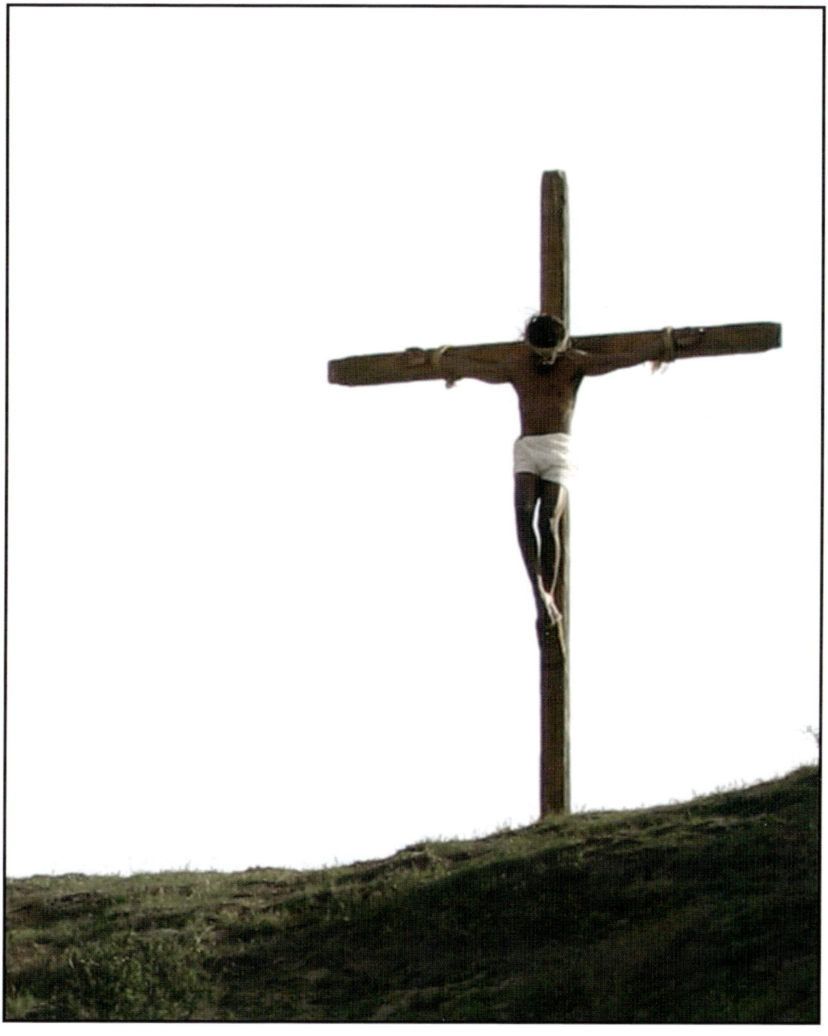

CRUCIFIXION OF A KING Chapter 23

One villager hands a Roman soldier a very large reed and he approaches my Master, who is swooning before him deliriously. He begins to beat my Master with the shaft, at first quite playfully, then gradually harder and harder. He hands the stick to one of his comrades so that they might join in the fun and they all begin to spit on my Master and hit him with their hands.

If my Master is knocked to the ground, one Centurion guard picks him up and holds him in place, much like a life-sized doll, so that others may kick and smack him until his face is bruised and swollen; much like the color of a salt-water lobster. The Romans only relent when my Master's body starts to spew blood uncontrollably, as they do not wish to kill him so early in the day.

They want him to suffer as terribly as possible. They wanted the crucifixion of the "self-proclaimed" Black King.

If I had not seen with my own eyes that it was my Master being stamped upon in such an agitated way, I swear that I would not have recognized him. The Messiah's face and body is marred beyond any person I have ever seen.

Then, a purple robe is offered up from within the crowd. Purple is the color of royalty, worn only by kings and queens. The cloth is extended to Horatius, who beckons the other guards to bring my Master forward. With no thought to the bloody ribbons of muscle hanging from my Master's back, Horatius cruelly wraps my Master ever so tightly in the elaborate material. My Master cries out in anguish and the Roman guards begin to taunt him.

The crowds part and the oversized guard that performed the lashings on my Master come towards him, dragging a crude, wooden cross. The guard stops in front of the spectacle and drops the cross onto the ground. The sound of it echoes throughout the town and the people become silent as they watch this symbolic occurrence.

The Centurion tells my Master that the wooden stake will be the last thing he will ever bear, and he is to carry the cross almost three miles to Golgotha.

I become infuriated when I hear the soldier say this.

It is obvious that my Master does not possess strength enough to carry the large cross even twelve paces, let alone three miles! He is already dying and depleted of blood and water, no doubt thirsty from the blistering sun's rays!

An anonymous villager has even taken the time to construct a "crown" to complete my Master's regal look. It is made up of twisted thorns and spiraling twigs, with the point of each barb facing inward. The towering guard raises the crown high above the Messiah's head, announcing to the world my Master's formal introduction as king.

"Here you have it Judea! It is the Messiah!" He grumbles.

"I present to you the King of the Jews!"

Without further ado, he plops the crown of thorns onto my Master's head, making sure to secure the sphere by sinking it deeply into my Master's forehead.

My Master has only strength enough to whimper pitifully, and the sound of it is high-pitched and forlorn; not unlike that of a kitten who has gotten his paw caught underneath a heavy wheelbarrow, crushing its bones from the weight of it.

The Centurions continue to harass my Master, forcing him towards the burden that signifies his death. He slowly walks to the place where the beams are lying and bends down with difficulty, attempting to lift the heavy pieces.

The material that is wrapped around my Master has become attached to his wounds, and the congealed flesh has hardened, fastening itself to his attire. As he stoops to secure the cross in his arms the folds of cloth became taut, and my Master yells out painfully as the cuts are re-opened. Finally, after many attempts, my Master is able to stand the bulky cross upright.

In this manner, my Master begins his journey towards Golgotha.

As the guards escort the Messiah to his fate, the oversized load is noticeably weakening my Master. The slabs of wood he holds are coarsely shaven and huge splinters are thrust into my Master's palms and fingers.

Trickles of blood run down his neck and face, and his only focus is on steadying the stout boards and continuing his steps. Whenever he stops to catch his breath he is pummeled in the mouth with the unyielding reed. His chapped lips crack, gathering fluid inside of the openings.

Not even one fourth of the way along the road to Golgotha, my Master succumbs to exhaustion and faints, toppling onto the earth. Horatius begins to kick and punch my Master in the stomach to wake him, but even his steel-toed boots and harrowing efforts do little to help my Master regain consciousness.

Has my Master possibly been trodden to death?

It would be a merciful accident, and I pray he does not wake from his fever.

Without warning my Master becomes alert, regurgitating blood and waste onto the terrain. He does not look as if he is able to walk even a foot further. How will he bear a huge cross for two more miles? The Romans are stumped, looking to one another for an answer. None of them wish to assume responsibility and cart the cross in the sweltering heat! But the guards know that my Master will not last if he is made to hold the heavy pieces.

Malchus, whom my Master had recently healed, points out a muscular man in the crowd.

"You there, what is your name and from where did you come?" he asks.

The man replies that his name is Simon and he travels from Cyrene. He is passing by on his way out of the country, and has become caught inside the shuffle of events. Malchus orders the man to pick up my Master's cross and bear it for him, in the name of Rome and Caesar. If he does not choose to comply with these orders, he will be arrested and likely imprisoned.

Upon hearing the severity of Malchus' threats, the Cyrenian agrees to take up the cross, although a disturbed look passes over his face. He goes to the place where my Master is lying and picks the burden up with ease, as if it had been a lighter load. He keeps his gaze downcast as he cannot stand the sight of my Master's suffering. The Romans continue to shove and push my Master in an attempt to revive him and continue the journey.

Taking pity upon my Master, Simon of Cyrene lays the cross down and helps my Master to his feet. It is the first and only motion of kindness that the Messiah has received today, and I am grateful for it. And although my Master is breathless and bloody, I do believe he is appreciative as well.

They continue down the path, all the while my Master looks more sickly. I have wiggled my way to the front of the crowd, and can clearly see my Master's face. I want to acknowledge him physically, but the Centurion's are too close for me to risk being spotted. At any rate, my Master's sight is so compromised that I hardly believe he will be able to recognize me.

We finally come to a small hill, and as we reach the top, all of what is called the "Place of a Skull" can be seen. This is where countless victims of crucifixion have been laid to rest. This is where my Master will finish his last breaths.

I shudder in anticipation.

Thoughts of escape run through my mind. I sorely wish that I had not followed my Master for all of these years, and broken bread with him season after season. Then I would have felt justified in leaving this gruesome scene. But I simply cannot abandon my Master any more than I already have. I am compelled to see our travels through until the end. And hopefully at the gates of Heaven's door, the Father will forgive me for my trespasses.

At last we begin to descend upon the area. As we come closer, two other men that have had judgment passed upon them come into view. They had been pierced and hung to die earlier that morning.

Reaching the clearing, Simon of Cyrene is directed to place my Master's cross in the center of the region. He sets the cross down swiftly and disappears into the crowd. He does not wish to participate further in the killing of my Master. He is gone before any of the guards can intercept him.

It takes three of the Roman guards to lift my Master's cross and place it firmly in the soil. They dig a moderately shallow hole for the base and sink the hilt of it into the earth. Then they pat the loose dirt back into position and proceed to assail my Master.

First, they callously strip my Master of his mauve colored robes, leaving him naked to the crowds once more. I gasp as his backside is put on display, for the bleeding is so profuse that it is a wonder he has not fainted once more. Horatius grabs my Master by the wrists and flings him towards the upright cross.

Then, one of the Romans opens a small box that holds an assortment of iron nails, all different lengths and widths. He takes three nails out of the box, all of which are approximately six inches long, and begins to sharpen them against a smooth stone. This causes a commotion from within the crowd; they are anticipating my Master's breathtaking finale!

I inspect the cross, wondering what it might feel like to be hanging from it. A few feet from the ground, a tiny board has been nailed to the cross as a footrest for my Master, the victim, for without it his pierced limbs might tear through the nails and his body will fall to the ground.

Then two of the guards raise my Master's body to the proper height and hold him in suspension, while the soldiers that have finished honing the iron pieces come towards the Messiah. The prophesied moment has arrived. My Master's betrayal and his elaborate capture by the Sanhedrin have boiled down to this very second.

Those who do not agree with the words my Master speaks and the truth that he reveals to all, have succeeded in quieting his teachings. It will not be long now.

Horatius curses at all of the soldiers. He has become hot and sweaty and is no longer amused with dragging out the crucifixion, no matter how many thousands of people are overlooking the hills. The guard holds my Master's feet so that he may strike both appendages at once, placing one leg on top of the other.

It is a wonder that my Master does not even make a sound as they force him onto the cross and I know he must be feeling something akin to relief that the end is nearing. Soon, he will be able to join the Father in heaven. The guard picks up a wooden mallet, his eyes squinting narrowly in the sunlight, and hammers the iron nail into my Master's feet.

My Master's screams resound in my ears and I see the blood gushing forth from his veins. The wooden step that his feet are resting on became bright and slippery and he shakes his head back and forth, as if trying to escape the pain.

Then, the Centurion guard holds his right arm against the panel and strikes another nail into his flesh, piercing it directly between the forearm and the pads of his hands. Wasting no time, he ruptures the left arm in the very same manner.

My Master is pinned to the cross, on display for all of Judea!

Immediately after witnessing all that they need to see, those that represent the Sanhedrin leave quickly, quill and parchment in hand, no doubt ready to relay the full details of his crucifixion to Caiaphus and the others.

The Roman guards each take another turn throwing rocks and teasing my

Master until Horatius puts a stop to all of that. The masses are ready to wreck havoc upon the Messiah as well and he is afraid that my Master may not live long enough to endure their attacks.

What insidious and corrupt reasoning the Romans lived by! They stop torturing the near dead only to prolong their suffering? My Master is already as good as gone. The people, then given the freedom to approach my Master, spit on him ferociously, quoting scriptures from the Torah as verbal ammunition against his teachings.

"You blasphemed all over Judea and thought you could get away with it, didn't you, Mighty King?" one sneers.

My Master does not reply. Instead, he looks up to the heavens, as if waiting for a response from the Father. His eyes are questioning, afraid. He asks the Father why he would leave the Messiah now, when all have abandoned my Master, while he is drowning in agony.

My Master is quite alone in his last hour.

Then, a woman can be heard calling out my Master's name, fighting her way through the masses until she reaches the clearing.

"Joshua!"

"Oh my son, what have they done to you?"

It is my Master's mother, Mary, and Mary Magdalene! Their presence alone is enough to revive my Master, and he attempts to smile down upon them.

Both women look worn and shaken; their faces drawn and grief-stricken. My Master speaks softly to his mother, Mary. He tells her that Mary of Magdalene, his most faithful of Disciples, is to be accepted and forgiven by his family from now on.

With tears overflowing, Mary agrees to her sons wishes.

Then, Mary Magdalene goes to where my Master is and speaks words up to him that only he can hear. I am certain that she whispers her love and devotion to him, promising above all things to carry his legacy and teachings on her shoulders. No matter how the conversation goes, my Master is pleased with Mary Magdalene. Instinctively, she reaches out to touch him but he declines her comfort, asking her to remember him as he was before, not as a dying martyr, struggling for every breath.

It seems that the crowd has witnessed enough bloodshed for one morning, and as the sun began to bake on all of our complexions, many head home to complete their daily chores. However, there are some ruthless citizens that long to plague my Master until the end.

One man in particular, Shamgar, will not leave the Messiah alone. He continues to slap my Master's legs and pull on his feet so that the flesh will tear painfully against the nails.

"Why don't you help yourself now, Nazareen?"

"Well, son of God? We're all waiting!"

"Leave him be!" My Master's mother interjects.

"Don't you think he's been tortured enough?" she cries out.

Then, friends of the cruel man join in on the riot, targeting Mary as well. They shove her in front of my Master and kick dirt into her eyes. A stout woman spits into Mary's hair, ridiculing her for claiming to have a virginal birth. They all hate my Master because he is a Black Nazareen. They are of the mind that he cannot be the Messiah because the possibility of God being Black is an insult to their intelligence.

They shout out that anyone who believes this imposter will burn in hell, just as my Master soon would!

Due to the heat and severe loss of blood, my Master begins to cry out for water. The Roman guard Malchus feels sympathy for my Master, and when Horatius is not looking, summons one of the others to dip a sponge into a glass of sour wine and put it to my Master's lips.

The guard squeezes a few drops of the wine into my Master's mouth and backs away from him. My Master looks to the sky, searching for a sign from the Father. Suddenly, for the first time since his capture, a look of tranquility comes over his face. The Messiah takes in a shallow breath, uttering these words.

"It is finished."

Then, his body becomes lifeless and his suffering is no more.

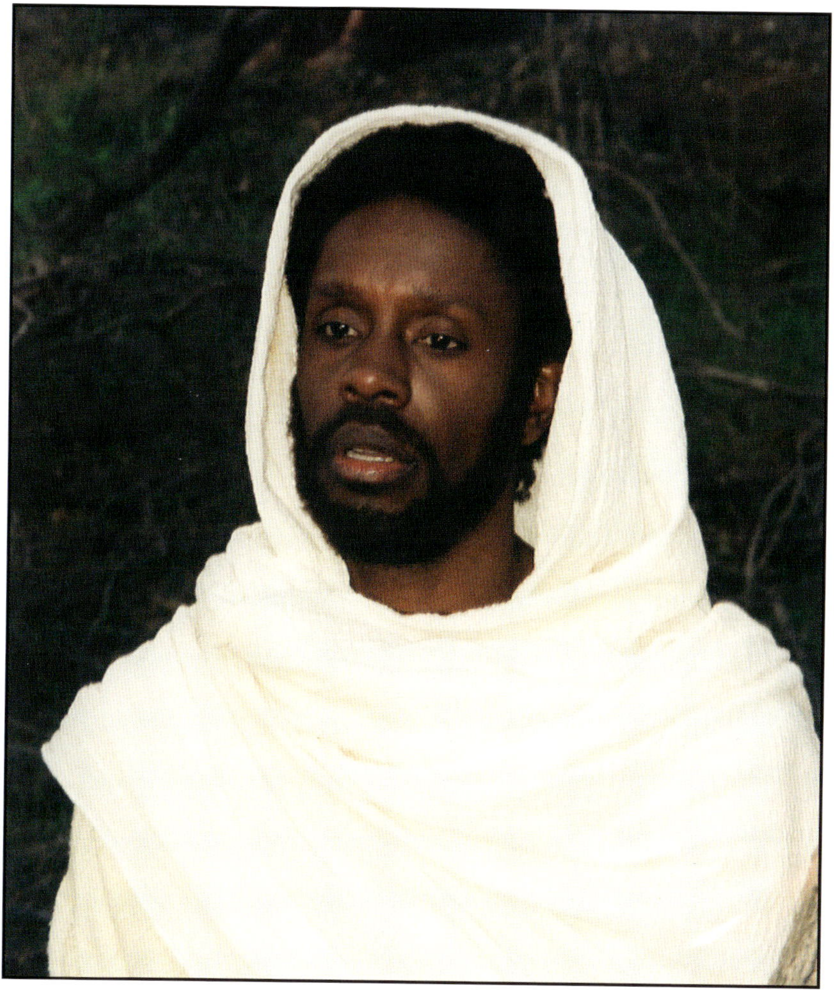

THE MESSIAH LIVES Chapter 24

We place him inside the tomb after it is mercifully all over with. The entire affair comes to me in bits and pieces, chaotic fragments strung together like colored seashells on a bit of yarn. I can still hear the crowds roaring, spitting, laughing at my Master.

I can feel the sinking of my stomach and hear the agonizing cries from a beautiful, abandoned soul. It seems the alliance of the Disciples is no more. We pray with one another after we seal his body inside the tomb, give our condolences to his earthly mother, and now part ways. It strikes me that we Disciples are but mere mortals walking our own paths, absorbed in our own embittered grief. Truly it is here, in the depths of my despairing, that I am able to wholly reflect on all that I have been part of.

The bonds we Disciples had forged over time became as durable as a towering stone fortress, coupled with the bravery of one hundred thousand loyal soldiers. I suppose, except for the traitor, Judas. Now, my brothers and I are as scattered as seeds in a dirt field, left to reproduce and flourish only according to our own devices.

This is the real test.

When there is no longer a shepherd to lead the herd, who will stray and who will follow the path of righteousness? When the mentor is watching only from above, will the protege live up to his full potential? Will we all spread the word and embrace his teachings for a lifetime, even in the midst of the offensive and corrupted world?

That is why I swear from this moment on to tell all who will listen of the Messiah's power and grace, that they may be enlightened and saved through him. I will carry out his legacy to the death, informing all of my Master's teachings and of his unparalleled kindness. Anything and everything I gain from this world shall be used to help those less fortunate, and to spread my Master's words to listening ears.

I must not doubt my Master now. The Father will look proudly upon his

Disciple, Thomas! I vow to do everything in my power to inform the masses of the Messiah's greatness. Those who seek to end my Master's words with the mutilation of his earthly body have failed.

My Master gave his life for all of us. He cared for us equally. From the lowly shepherds and prostitutes to the greatest teacher of his words, my Master loved all, even the Sanhedrin and the Romans. His was that of an unconditional love, one not of this planet.

My Master, Joshua of Nazareth, gave his life for the nations to be spared, and I am here to make certain the world will know of it, for many ages to come. Through his words, the Messiah will live forever.

Thomas the Fisherman,
Beloved disciple of Joshua of Nazareth, King of the Jews

I pray that I may never have doubt again....

122 Color Of The Cross

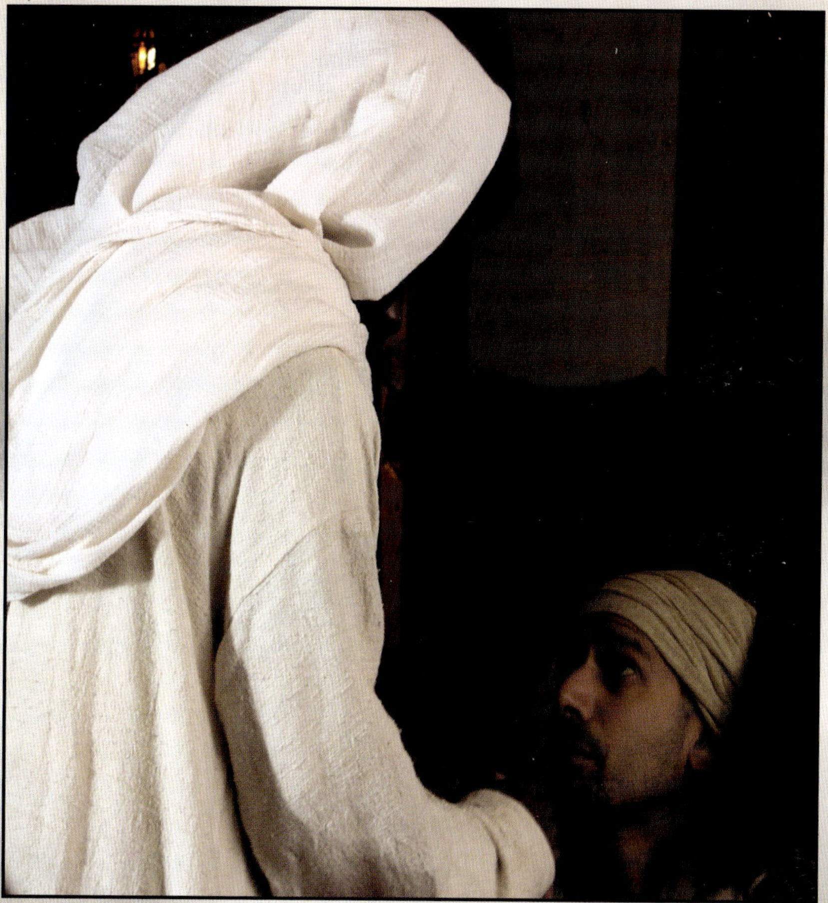

SPECIAL THANKS

BlackChristianMovies.com

Printing By:
LA Modem / Jean Paul Nataf
LAmodem.com

Editing By:
Marvin Wethington

Movie Stills Photography By:
Teddi Brown

Additional Photography By:
veroniquephoto.com